MODULE FOUR
Book 1
Answers

Notes on all the 'Let's investigate' sections
will be found in the Teacher's Resource Book.

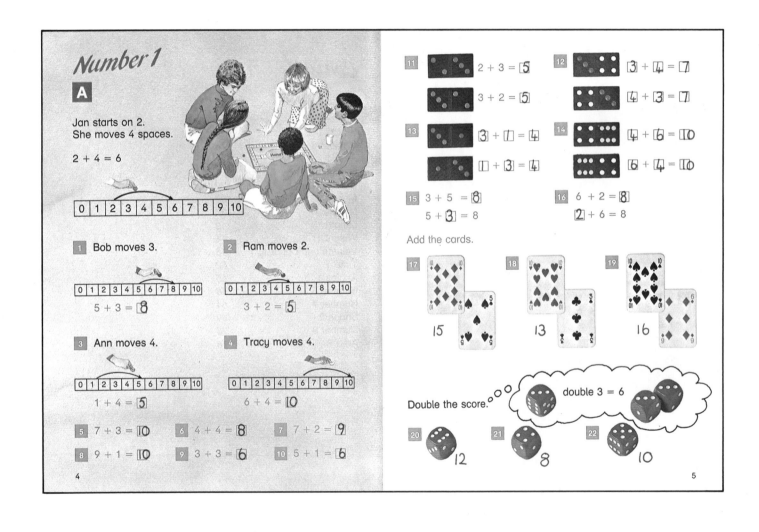

Number 1

A

Jan starts on 2.
She moves 4 spaces.

$2 + 4 = 6$

| 0 | 1 | 2 | 3 | 4 | 5 | 6 | 7 | 8 | 9 | 10 |

1 Bob moves 3.

| 0 | 1 | 2 | 3 | 4 | 5 | 6 | 7 | 8 | 9 | 10 |

$5 + 3 = 8$

2 Ram moves 2.

| 0 | 1 | 2 | 3 | 4 | 5 | 6 | 7 | 8 | 9 | 10 |

$3 + 2 = 5$

3 Ann moves 4.

| 0 | 1 | 2 | 3 | 4 | 5 | 6 | 7 | 8 | 9 | 10 |

$1 + 4 = 5$

4 Tracy moves 4.

| 0 | 1 | 2 | 3 | 4 | 5 | 6 | 7 | 8 | 9 | 10 |

$6 + 4 = 10$

5 $7 + 3 = 10$ **6** $4 + 4 = 8$ **7** $7 + 2 = 9$

8 $9 + 1 = 10$ **9** $3 + 3 = 6$ **10** $5 + 1 = 6$

4

11 $2 + 3 = 5$ **12** $3 + 4 = 7$

$3 + 2 = 5$ $4 + 3 = 7$

13 $3 + 1 = 4$ **14** $4 + 6 = 10$

$1 + 3 = 4$ $6 + 4 = 10$

15 $3 + 5 = 8$ **16** $6 + 2 = 8$

$5 + 3 = 8$ $2 + 6 = 8$

Add the cards.

17 15   **18** 13   **19** 16

Double the score.   double 3 = 6

20 12   **21** 8   **22** 10

5

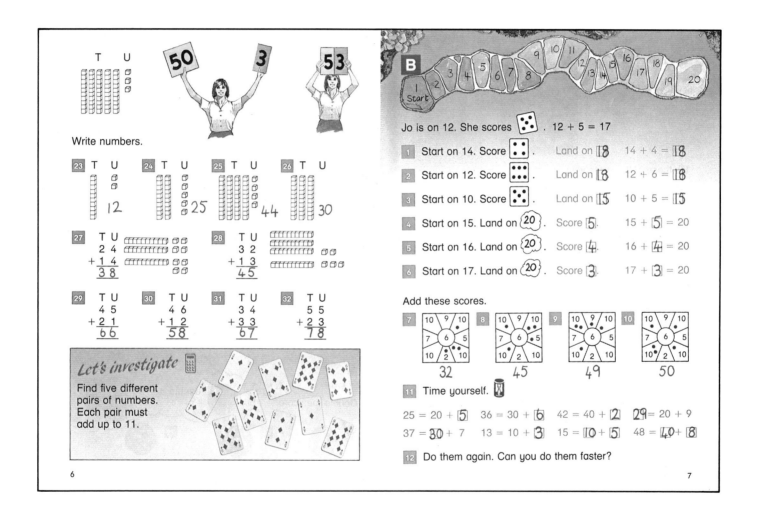

T U

50 3 53

Write numbers.

23 T U 12
24 T U 25
25 T U 44
26 T U 30

27 T U
2 4
+1 4
3 8

28 T U
3 2
+1 3
4 5

29 T U
4 5
+2 1
6 6

30 T U
4 6
+1 2
5 8

31 T U
3 4
+3 3
6 7

32 T U
5 5
+2 3
7 8

Let's investigate

Find five different pairs of numbers. Each pair must add up to 11.

B

Jo is on 12. She scores [dice]. 12 + 5 = 17

1 Start on 14. Score [dice]. Land on [1]8 14 + 4 = [1]8

2 Start on 12. Score [dice]. Land on [1]8 12 + 6 = [1]8

3 Start on 10. Score [dice]. Land on [1]5 10 + 5 = [1]5

4 Start on 15. Land on (20). Score [5]. 15 + [5] = 20

5 Start on 16. Land on (20). Score [4]. 16 + [4] = 20

6 Start on 17. Land on (20). Score [3]. 17 + [3] = 20

Add these scores.

7 32 **8** 45 **9** 49 **10** 50

11 Time yourself.

25 = 20 + [5]   36 = 30 + [6]   42 = 40 + [2]   2[9] = 20 + 9

37 = [3]0 + 7   13 = 10 + [3]   15 = [1]0 + [5]   48 = [4]0 + [8]

12 Do them again. Can you do them faster?

6
7

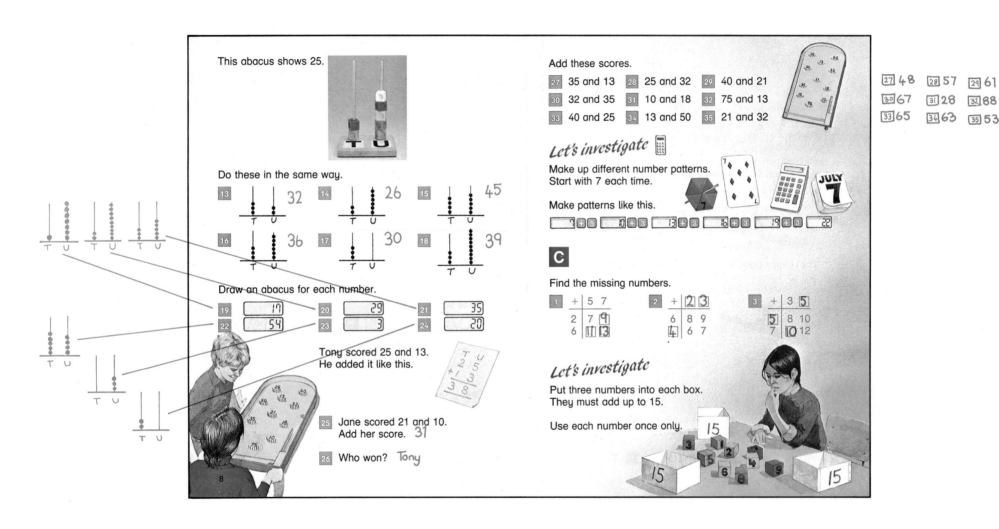

This abacus shows 25.

Do these in the same way.

13   32
14   26
15   45
16   36
17   30
18   39

Draw an abacus for each number.

19   17
22   54
20   29
23   3
21   35
24   20

Tony scored 25 and 13.
He added it like this.

T U
2 5
+1 3
3 8

25   Jane scored 21 and 10.
Add her score.   31

26   Who won?   Tony

Add these scores.

27   35 and 13
28   25 and 32
29   40 and 21
30   32 and 35
31   10 and 18
32   75 and 13
33   40 and 25
34   13 and 50
35   21 and 32

27   48   28   57   29   61
30   67   31   28   32   68
33   65   34   63   35   53

Let's investigate

Make up different number patterns.
Start with 7 each time.

Make patterns like this.

7 + 3   10 + 3   13 + 3   16 + 3   19 + 3   22

C

Find the missing numbers.

1   + | 5 7
    2 | 7 9
    6 | 11 13

2   + | 2 3
    6 | 8 9
    4 | 6 7

3   + | 3 5
    5 | 8 10
    7 | 10 12

Let's investigate

Put three numbers into each box.
They must add up to 15.

Use each number once only.

15
15
15

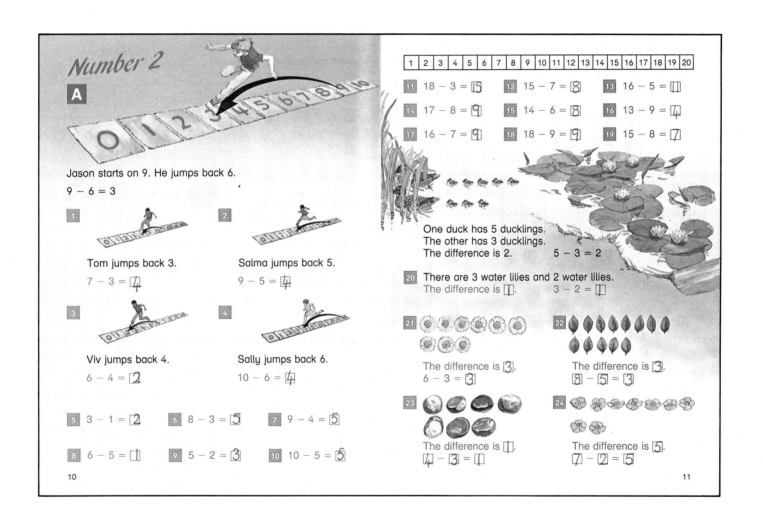

Number 2

A

Jason starts on 9. He jumps back 6.

$9 - 6 = 3$

1

2

Tom jumps back 3.

$7 - 3 = \boxed{4}$

Salma jumps back 5.

$9 - 5 = \boxed{4}$

3

4

Viv jumps back 4.

$6 - 4 = \boxed{2}$

Sally jumps back 6.

$10 - 6 = \boxed{4}$

5 $3 - 1 = \boxed{2}$ **6** $8 - 3 = \boxed{5}$ **7** $9 - 4 = \boxed{5}$

8 $6 - 5 = \boxed{1}$ **9** $5 - 2 = \boxed{3}$ **10** $10 - 5 = \boxed{5}$

10

| 1 | 2 | 3 | 4 | 5 | 6 | 7 | 8 | 9 | 10 | 11 | 12 | 13 | 14 | 15 | 16 | 17 | 18 | 19 | 20 |

11 $18 - 3 = \boxed{15}$ **12** $15 - 7 = \boxed{8}$ **13** $16 - 5 = \boxed{11}$

14 $17 - 8 = \boxed{9}$ **15** $14 - 6 = \boxed{8}$ **16** $13 - 9 = \boxed{4}$

17 $16 - 7 = \boxed{9}$ **18** $18 - 9 = \boxed{9}$ **19** $15 - 8 = \boxed{7}$

One duck has 5 ducklings.
The other has 3 ducklings.
The difference is 2. $5 - 3 = 2$

20 There are 3 water lilies and 2 water lilies.
The difference is $\boxed{1}$. $3 - 2 = \boxed{1}$

21

The difference is $\boxed{3}$.
$6 - 3 = \boxed{3}$

22

The difference is $\boxed{3}$.
$\boxed{8} - \boxed{5} = \boxed{3}$

23

The difference is $\boxed{1}$.
$\boxed{4} - \boxed{3} = \boxed{1}$

24

The difference is $\boxed{5}$.
$\boxed{7} - \boxed{2} = \boxed{5}$

11

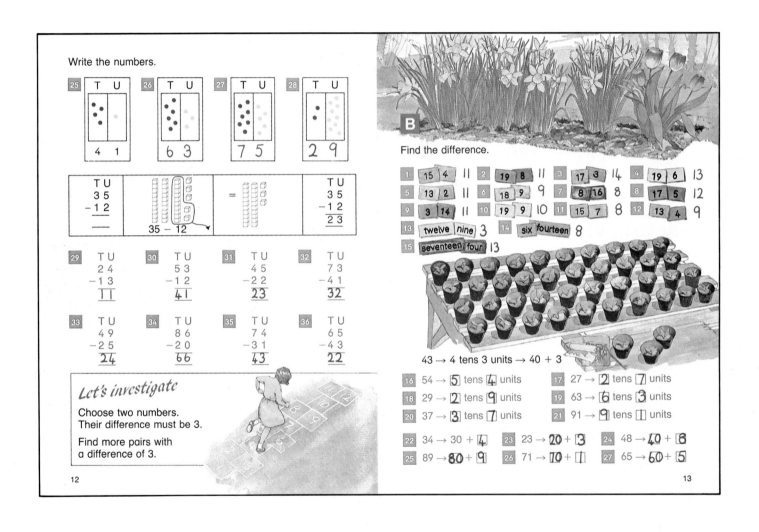

Write the numbers.

25 T U	26 T U	27 T U	28 T U
4 1	6 3	7 5	2 9

T U			T U
3 5		=	3 5
− 1 2			− 1 2
	35 − 12		2 3

29 T U	30 T U	31 T U	32 T U
2 4	5 3	4 5	7 3
− 1 3	− 1 2	− 2 2	− 4 1
11	41	23	32

33 T U	34 T U	35 T U	36 T U
4 9	8 6	7 4	6 5
− 2 5	− 2 0	− 3 1	− 4 3
24	66	43	22

Let's investigate

Choose two numbers.
Their difference must be 3.

Find more pairs with
a difference of 3.

B

Find the difference.

1 15 4 11 2 19 8 11 3 17 3 14 4 19 6 13

5 13 2 11 6 18 9 9 7 8 16 8 8 17 5 12

9 3 14 11 10 19 9 10 11 15 7 8 12 13 4 9

13 twelve nine 3 14 six fourteen 8

15 seventeen four 13

43 → 4 tens 3 units → 40 + 3

16 54 → 5 tens 4 units   17 27 → 2 tens 7 units

18 29 → 2 tens 9 units   19 63 → 6 tens 3 units

20 37 → 3 tens 7 units   21 91 → 9 tens 1 units

22 34 → 30 + 4   23 23 → 20 + 3   24 48 → 40 + 8

25 89 → 80 + 9   26 71 → 70 + 1   27 65 → 60 + 5

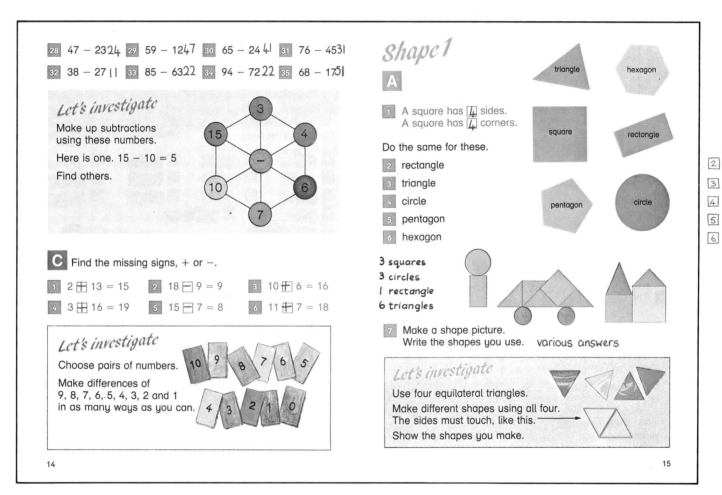

28 47 − 23 24   **29** 59 − 12 47   **30** 65 − 24 41   **31** 76 − 45 31

32 38 − 27 11   **33** 85 − 63 22   **34** 94 − 72 22   **35** 68 − 17 51

Let's investigate

Make up subtractions using these numbers.

Here is one. 15 − 10 = 5

Find others.

C Find the missing signs, + or −.

1 2 ⊞ 13 = 15   **2** 18 ⊟ 9 = 9   **3** 10 ⊞ 6 = 16

4 3 ⊞ 16 = 19   **5** 15 ⊟ 7 = 8   **6** 11 ⊞ 7 = 18

Let's investigate

Choose pairs of numbers.

Make differences of
9, 8, 7, 6, 5, 4, 3, 2 and 1
in as many ways as you can.

Shape 1

A

1 A square has [4] sides.
A square has [4] corners.

Do the same for these.

2 rectangle
3 triangle
4 circle
5 pentagon
6 hexagon

	sides	corners
2	4	4
3	3	3
4	1	0
5	5	5
6	6	6

3 squares
3 circles
1 rectangle
6 triangles

7 Make a shape picture.
Write the shapes you use.   various answers

Let's investigate

Use four equilateral triangles.

Make different shapes using all four.
The sides must touch, like this. →

Show the shapes you make.

14

15

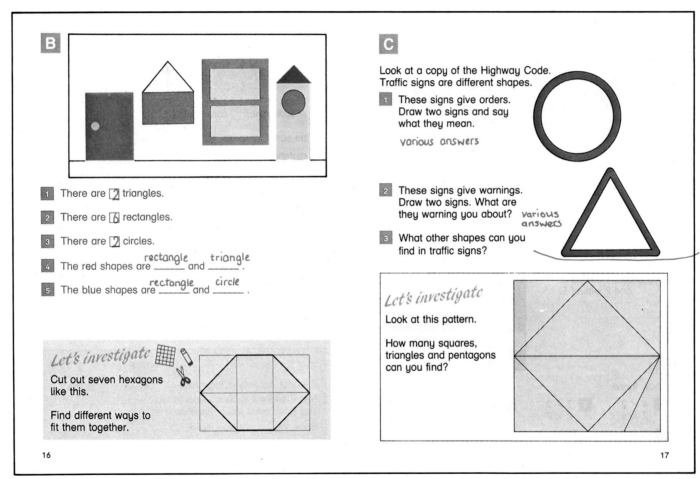

B

1 There are ☐2 triangles.

2 There are ☐6 rectangles.

3 There are ☐2 circles.

4 The red shapes are _rectangle_ and _triangle_.

5 The blue shapes are _rectangle_ and _circle_.

Let's investigate

Cut out seven hexagons like this.

Find different ways to fit them together.

16

C

Look at a copy of the Highway Code. Traffic signs are different shapes.

1 These signs give orders. Draw two signs and say what they mean.

   various answers

2 These signs give warnings. Draw two signs. What are they warning you about?   *various answers*

3 What other shapes can you find in traffic signs?

   various answers including rectangles, squares, octagons (see the Highway Code)

Let's investigate

Look at this pattern.

How many squares, triangles and pentagons can you find?

17

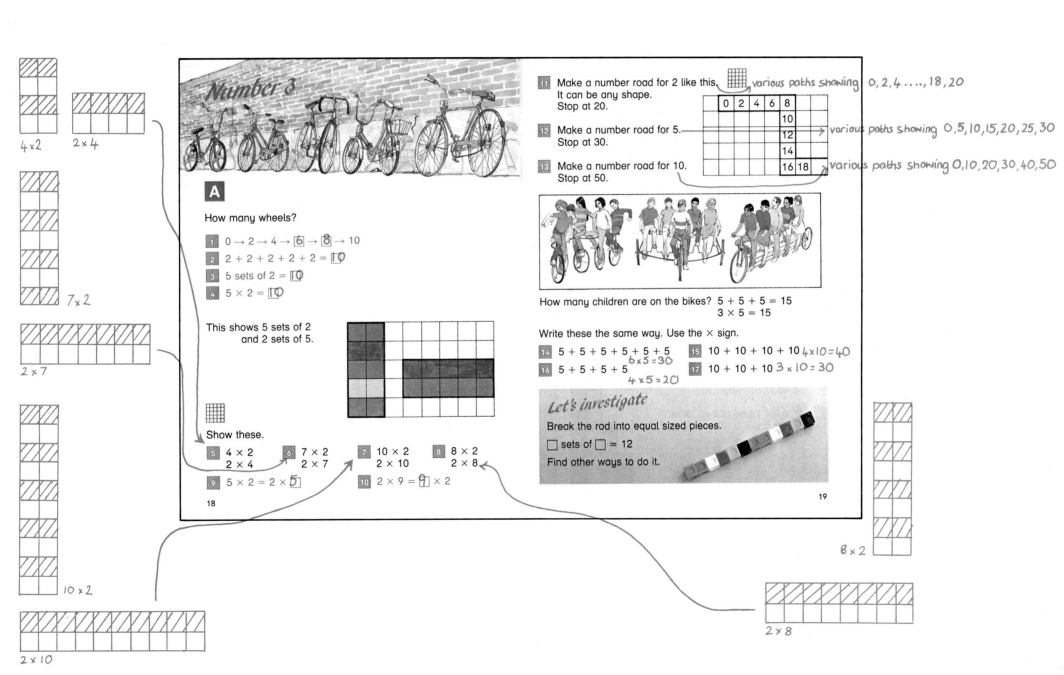

Number 3

A

How many wheels?

1. $0 \to 2 \to 4 \to \boxed{6} \to \boxed{8} \to 10$
2. $2 + 2 + 2 + 2 + 2 = \boxed{10}$
3. 5 sets of $2 = \boxed{10}$
4. $5 \times 2 = \boxed{10}$

This shows 5 sets of 2
and 2 sets of 5.

Show these.

5. 4×2
   2×4
6. 7×2
   2×7
7. 10×2
   2×10
8. 8×2
   2×8
9. $5 \times 2 = 2 \times \boxed{5}$
10. $2 \times 9 = \boxed{9} \times 2$

18

11. Make a number road for 2 like this. various paths showing 0,2,4...,18,20
    It can be any shape.
    Stop at 20.
12. Make a number road for 5. various paths showing 0,5,10,15,20,25,30
    Stop at 30.
13. Make a number road for 10. various paths showing 0,10,20,30,40,50
    Stop at 50.

0	2	4	6	8		
				10		
				12		
				14		
				16	18	

How many children are on the bikes? $5 + 5 + 5 = 15$
$3 \times 5 = 15$

Write these the same way. Use the $\times$ sign.

14. $5 + 5 + 5 + 5 + 5 + 5$ $6 \times 5 = 30$
15. $10 + 10 + 10 + 10$ $4 \times 10 = 40$
16. $5 + 5 + 5 + 5$ $4 \times 5 = 20$
17. $10 + 10 + 10$ $3 \times 10 = 30$

Let's investigate

Break the rod into equal sized pieces.

$\square$ sets of $\square = 12$

Find other ways to do it.

19

4×2 2×4 7×2 2×7 10×2 2×10 8×2 2×8

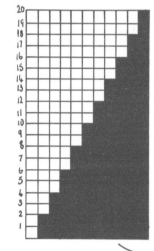

B

Suzy gave 2 oranges to each of her four friends.

$2 + 2 + 2 + 2 = 8$ oranges $4 \times 2 = 8$

1 Duncan eats 2 bananas every day.
How many bananas does he eat in a week? 14

2
🍒🍒 2 cherries $1 \times 2 = 2$

🍒🍒 🍒🍒 $2 + 2 = 4$ cherries $2 \times 2 = 4$

🍒🍒 🍒🍒 🍒🍒 $2 + 2 + 2 = 6$ cherries $3 \times 2 = 6$

Go up to 10 pairs of cherries.

3 Draw a graph of the table of 2, like this.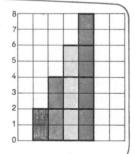
Go up to 20.

4 Write the tables of 2 as far as 10×2 and 2×10.

$1 \times 2 = \square$ $2 \times 1 = \square$
$2 \times 2 = \square$ $2 \times 2 = \square$
$3 \times 2 = \square$ $2 \times 3 = \square$
$4 \times 2 = \square$ $2 \times 4 = \square$
continue   continue
20 to $10 \times 2 = 20$ to $2 \times 10 = 20$

This number line shows
$2 + 2 + 2 + 2 = 4 \times 2 = 8$
$4 + 4 = 2 \times 4 = 8$

What do these lines show?

5

$2 + 2 + 2 + 2 + 2 = 5 \times 2 = 10$ $5 + 5 = 2 \times 5 = 10$

6

$5 + 5 + 5 = 3 \times 5 = 15$
$3 + 3 + 3 + 3 + 3 = 5 \times 3 = 15$

7 Draw a number line to show 3×10 and 10×3.

Let's investigate

Here are some apples.
Find ways to make equal groups.

Find numbers between 10 and 20 that cannot be put into equal groups.

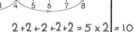

C Find the missing numbers.

	3	5	6	1	7	2	0	10	4	8
× 5	15	25	30	5	35	10	0	50	20	40
× 2	6	10	12	2	14	4	0	20	8	16
× 10	30	50	60	10	70	20	0	100	40	80

Let's investigate

Find ways of making 18. Use 2, 3, 6, 9, +, ×.

21

🍒🍒 🍒🍒 🍒🍒 $2 + 2 + 2 + 2 = 8$ cherries $4 \times 2 = 8$

continue to...

🍒🍒 🍒🍒 🍒🍒 🍒🍒 🍒🍒 🍒🍒 🍒🍒 🍒🍒 🍒🍒 🍒🍒 $2 + 2 + 2 + 2 + 2 + 2 + 2 + 2 + 2 + 2 = 20$ cherries $10 \times 2 = 20$

Area 1

A

1. Cover a book with squares of the same size.
Do squares cover well? Yes

2. Cover the book with rectangles.
Do rectangles cover well? Yes

3. Cover the book with circles.
Do circles cover well? No

square

rectangle

circle

Let's investigate

Draw shapes.
Use five squares each time.
The sides must fit like this.
How many different shapes can you make?

B

1. Draw round an equilateral triangle.
Draw some more.
Are equilateral triangles good for covering? Yes

22

square   circle   pentagon   hexagon   rectangle   equilateral triangle

2. Draw round some other shapes.
Which ones cover well? hexagon, square, rectangle, equilateral triangle

3. Look at these shapes.
What will you use to cover them? Square

The square covers the shapes best.

Let's investigate

Draw different rectangles which cover 12 squares.

C Let's investigate

Draw a rectangle like this.
Find ways of dividing it into squares of the same size.

Draw a bigger rectangle that you can divide into squares.

23

Number 4

A

Put 12 children in 2 teams.

$12 \div 2 = 6$ in each team.

1 Put 12 children in 3 teams. $12 \div 3 = 4$
2 Put 12 children in 4 teams. $12 \div 4 = 3$

Share the things equally.

3 $9 \div 3 = 3$

4 $8 \div 2 = 4$

1	2
3	4
5	6
7	8
9	10
11	12
13	14
15	16

1	2	3
4	5	6
7	8	9
10	11	12
13	14	15
16	17	18
19	20	21
22	23	24

1	2	3	4
5	6	7	8
9	10	11	12
13	14	15	16
17	18	19	20
21	22	23	24
25	26	27	28
29	30	31	32

1	2	3	4	5
6	7	8	9	10
11	12	13	14	15
16	17	18	19	20
21	22	23	24	25
26	27	28	29	30
31	32	33	34	35
36	37	38	39	40

Use the charts.

5 $16 \div 2 = 8$
  $12 \div 2 = 6$
  $8 \div 2 = 4$
  $14 \div 2 = 7$

6 $24 \div 3 = 8$
  $12 \div 3 = 4$
  $21 \div 3 = 7$
  $18 \div 3 = 6$

7 $20 \div 4 = 5$
  $28 \div 4 = 7$
  $12 \div 4 = 3$
  $32 \div 4 = 8$

8 $40 \div 5 = 8$
  $30 \div 5 = 6$
  $15 \div 5 = 3$
  $35 \div 5 = 7$

Let's investigate

Find ways to divide 12.
Write down your ways.

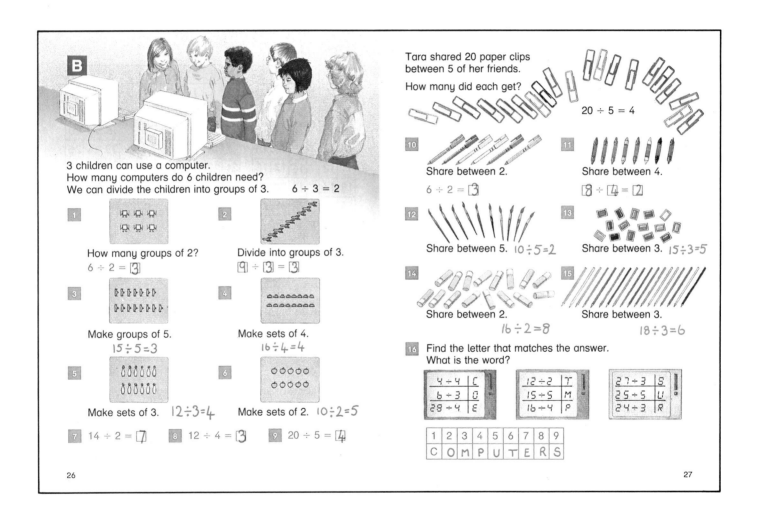

B

3 children can use a computer.
How many computers do 6 children need?
We can divide the children into groups of 3.   6 ÷ 3 = 2

1

How many groups of 2?
6 ÷ 2 = 3

2

Divide into groups of 3.
9 ÷ 3 = 3

3

Make groups of 5.
15 ÷ 5 = 3

4

Make sets of 4.
16 ÷ 4 = 4

5

Make sets of 3. 12 ÷ 3 = 4

6

Make sets of 2. 10 ÷ 2 = 5

7 14 ÷ 2 = 7   **8** 12 ÷ 4 = 3   **9** 20 ÷ 5 = 4

26

Tara shared 20 paper clips
between 5 of her friends.

How many did each get?

20 ÷ 5 = 4

10

Share between 2.
6 ÷ 2 = 3

11

Share between 4.
8 ÷ 4 = 2

12

Share between 5. 10 ÷ 5 = 2

13

Share between 3. 15 ÷ 3 = 5

14

Share between 2.
16 ÷ 2 = 8

15

Share between 3.
18 ÷ 3 = 6

16 Find the letter that matches the answer.
What is the word?

4 ÷ 4	C
6 ÷ 3	O
28 ÷ 4	E

12 ÷ 2	T
15 ÷ 5	M
16 ÷ 4	P

27 ÷ 3	S
25 ÷ 5	U
24 ÷ 3	R

1	2	3	4	5	6	7	8	9
C	O	M	P	U	T	E	R	S

27

Let's investigate

Kathy can make four number sentences using 2, 3, 6, ×, ÷, =.

$3 \times 2 = 6$
$2 \times 3 = 6$
$6 \div 3 = 2$
$6 \div 2 = 3$

Do the same for these.

C Let's investigate

Yasmin's computer makes number sentences using the number 12.

How many can you make?

28

Data 1

A

Some children went for a walk.

They saw these animals.

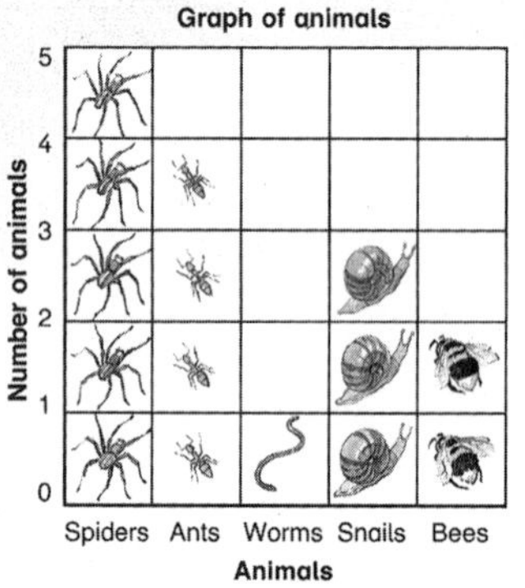

Graph of animals

1 Draw a block graph like this.

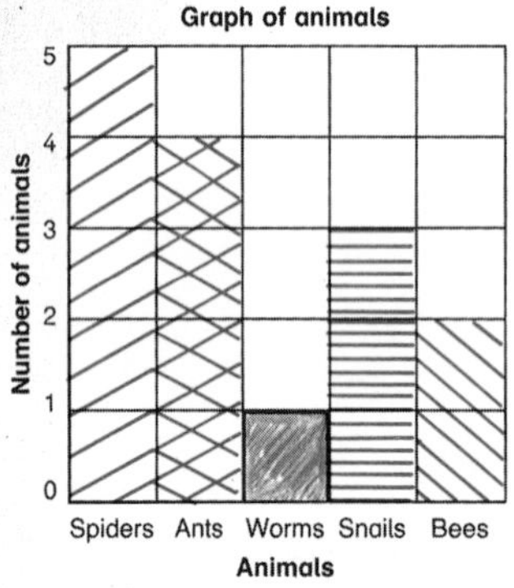

Graph of animals

2 How many spiders are there? 5

3 How many snails are there? 3

4 How many more ants than bees are there? 2

29

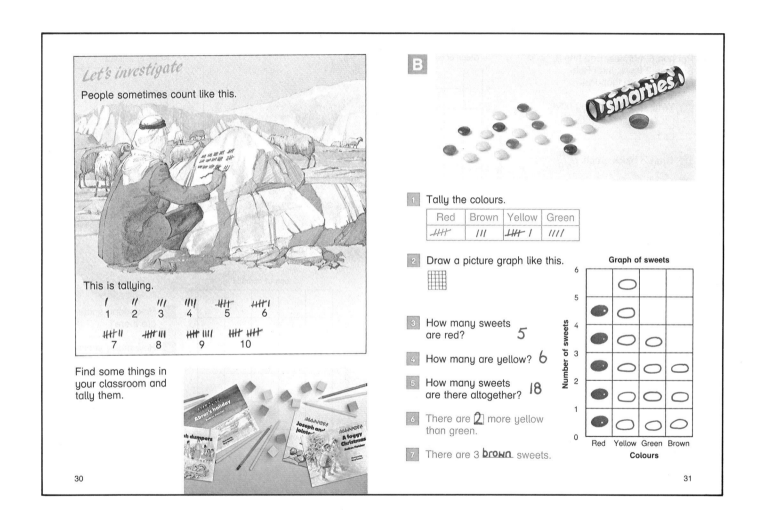

Let's investigate

People sometimes count like this.

This is tallying.

| / | // | /// | //// | ////| | ////// |
| 1 | 2 | 3 | 4 | 5 | 6 |

| ////// | ////// | ///// //// | ////// ////// |
| 7 | 8 | 9 | 10 |

Find some things in your classroom and tally them.

30

B

1 Tally the colours.

Red	Brown	Yellow	Green
////	///	//// /	////

2 Draw a picture graph like this.

Graph of sweets

3 How many sweets are red?   5

4 How many are yellow?   6

5 How many sweets are there altogether?   18

6 There are 2 more yellow than green.

7 There are 3 **brown** sweets.

31

Pat has 6 marbles. Bob has 8.
Sue has 2 fewer than Bob.
Liz has 1 more than Pat.

8 Write how many they have.

Bob	Sue	Pat	Liz
8	6	6	7

9 Draw a block graph.

10 Who has the most marbles? Bob

11 Who has 6? Sue and Pat

12 Sue and Liz have 13 altogether.

Let's investigate

Ask 10 friends their favourite day.

Make a tally. Draw a graph.

C *Let's investigate*

Nicky has the most. Mark has the least.
Laura has 2 more than Mark.
Sophie has more than Laura.

Draw different graphs for this.
Choose titles and labels for your graphs.

32

Graph of marbles

Number of marbles (y-axis: 0–10)
Children (x-axis: Bob, Sue, Pat, Liz)

Money 1

A

1 You need these coins.

Put the coins in order.
Start with 1p.
Draw round them.

Count the money.

2 8 p

3 17 p

4 26 p

5 29 p

6 15 p

What coins are needed? Draw them.

7 6p 5 1

8 9p 5 2 2

9 12p 10 2

10 15p 10 5

11 25p 20 5

12 30p 20 10

33

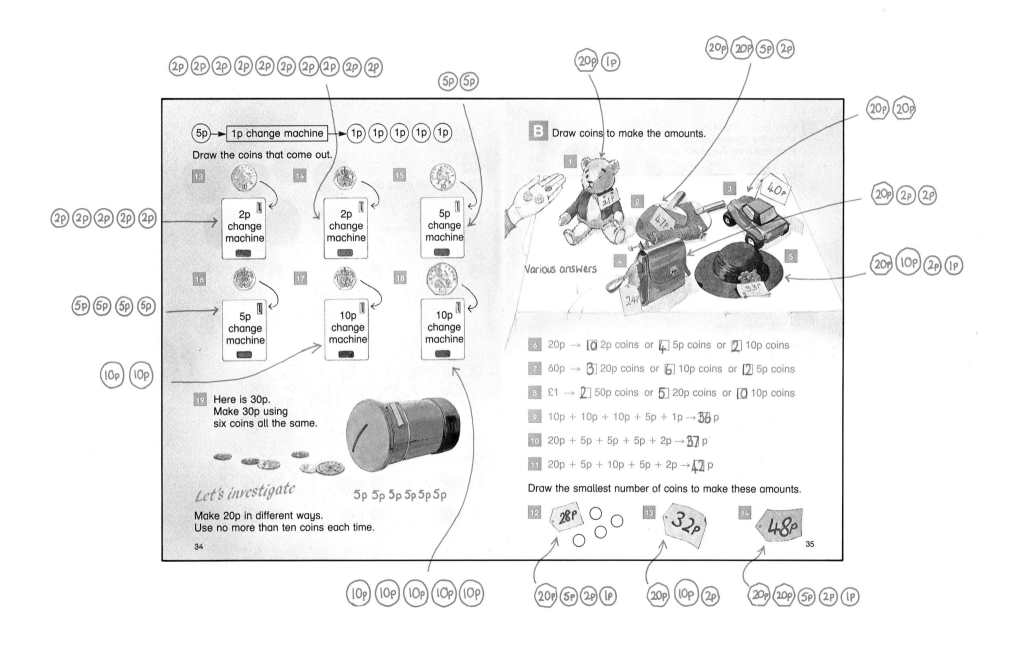

(5p) → [1p change machine] → (1p)(1p)(1p)(1p)(1p)

Draw the coins that come out.

13   2p change machine

14   2p change machine

15   5p change machine

16   5p change machine

17   10p change machine

18   10p change machine

19 Here is 30p.
Make 30p using
six coins all the same.

Let's investigate

5p 5p 5p 5p 5p 5p

Make 20p in different ways.
Use no more than ten coins each time.

34

B Draw coins to make the amounts.

1   2

3

4   5

Various answers

6   20p → [10] 2p coins or [4] 5p coins or [2] 10p coins

7   60p → [3] 20p coins or [6] 10p coins or [12] 5p coins

8   £1 → [2] 50p coins or [5] 20p coins or [10] 10p coins

9   10p + 10p + 10p + 5p + 1p → [36] p

10 20p + 5p + 5p + 5p + 2p → [37] p

11 20p + 5p + 10p + 5p + 2p → [42] p

Draw the smallest number of coins to make these amounts.

12 28P

13 32P

14 48P

35

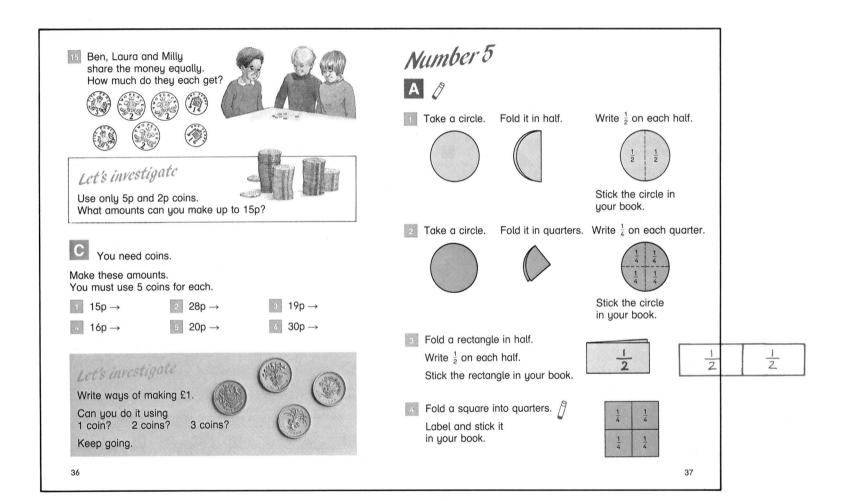

15 Ben, Laura and Milly
share the money equally.
How much do they each get?

Let's investigate

Use only 5p and 2p coins.
What amounts can you make up to 15p?

C   You need coins.

Make these amounts.
You must use 5 coins for each.

1 15p →   2 28p →   3 19p →

4 16p →   5 20p →   6 30p →

Let's investigate

Write ways of making £1.

Can you do it using
1 coin?   2 coins?   3 coins?

Keep going.

1 10 2 1 1 1
   5 5 2 2 1
2 20 2 2 2 2
   20 5 1 1 1
   10 10 5 2 1
3 10 5 2 1 1
   5 5 5 2 2
4 10 2 2 1 1
   5 5 2 2 2
5 10 5 2 2 1
6 20 5 2 2 1

Number 5

A

1 Take a circle.   Fold it in half.   Write ½ on each half.

Stick the circle in
your book.

2 Take a circle.   Fold it in quarters.   Write ¼ on each quarter.

Stick the circle
in your book.

3 Fold a rectangle in half.

Write ½ on each half.

Stick the rectangle in your book.

1/2

1/2	1/2

4 Fold a square into quarters.

Label and stick it
in your book.

1/4	1/4
1/4	1/4

36   37

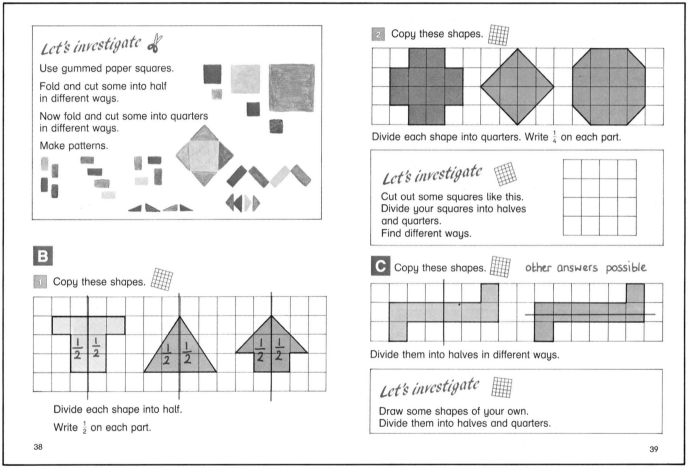

Let's investigate ✂

Use gummed paper squares.

Fold and cut some into half in different ways.

Now fold and cut some into quarters in different ways.

Make patterns.

B

1 Copy these shapes.

Divide each shape into half.

Write $\frac{1}{2}$ on each part.

38

2 Copy these shapes.

Divide each shape into quarters. Write $\frac{1}{4}$ on each part.

Let's investigate

Cut out some squares like this.
Divide your squares into halves and quarters.
Find different ways.

C Copy these shapes.   other answers possible

Divide them into halves in different ways.

Let's investigate

Draw some shapes of your own.
Divide them into halves and quarters.

39

Length 1

A

The Ancient Egyptians measured things using parts of their body. One part was the cubit. Cubit rulers were made from metal bars. These were used to help build the pyramids.

You can measure with parts of your body. You can use your cubit, span and digit.

cubit

span

Measure with your span.

1
2
3   digits

See if your friend has the same answers.

Measure with your cubit.   Measure with your digit.

4   The bookcase is ☐ cubits long.   6   My pencil is ☐ digits long.

5   The cupboard is ☐ cubits wide.   7   The book is ☐ digits wide.

8   My ruler is ☐ digits long.

Various answers

Various answers

40

41

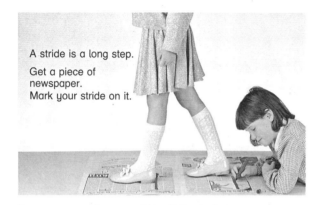

A stride is a long step.

Get a piece of newspaper.
Mark your stride on it.

Now measure using your stride. Estimate first.

	Estimate	Measure
9 Classroom length		
10 Corridor length		
11 Playground length		

12 Is your stride the same as your friend's?
Is it longer or shorter?

Let's investigate

Choose some things to measure.

What will you measure them in?

B

A long time ago, people said a man's height was about the same as his reach.

Your reach is from fingertips to fingertips.

Use the picture to help you.

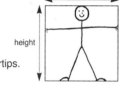
reach

height

1 Draw a stickman with a reach of 6 digits.
Write his height.

2 Draw another stickman with a reach of 10 digits.
Write his height.

3 Which stickman is taller?

The 10 digit stick man

Let's investigate

Do the taller children in your class have longer reaches?

Measure some of your friends to find out.

C *Let's investigate*

Find out how many of your digits measure your span.
How many of your spans measure your cubit?
How many of your cubits measure your stride?
How many of your spans measure your reach?

Do you get the same answers as anyone else?

Various answers

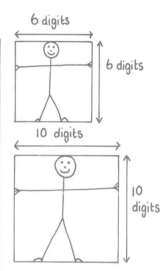

6 digits

6 digits

10 digits

10 digits

42

43

Weight 1

A

lighter
box
tin
heavier
scales
scissors   feather   ruler   stone   tin

1   Is the tin heavier than the box?

2   Is the stone lighter than the scissors?

3   Is the ruler heavier or lighter than the box?

Use all the things.

4   The heaviest is _____ .

5   The lightest is _____ .

Answers depend on the apparatus supplied

6   Put all the things in order.
    Start with the heaviest.

cup   box   plasticine   cubes   spoon

7   ☐ cubes balance the cup.

8   ☐ cubes balance the spoon.

9   ☐ cubes balance the box.

10 ☐ cubes balance the plasticine.

11 The lightest is the _____ .

Answers depend on the apparatus supplied

Let's investigate

Find some small things that are heavy.

Find some large things that are light.

Ask your friends to guess the heavy things.
They may look but not touch.

Answers depend on
the apparatus
supplied

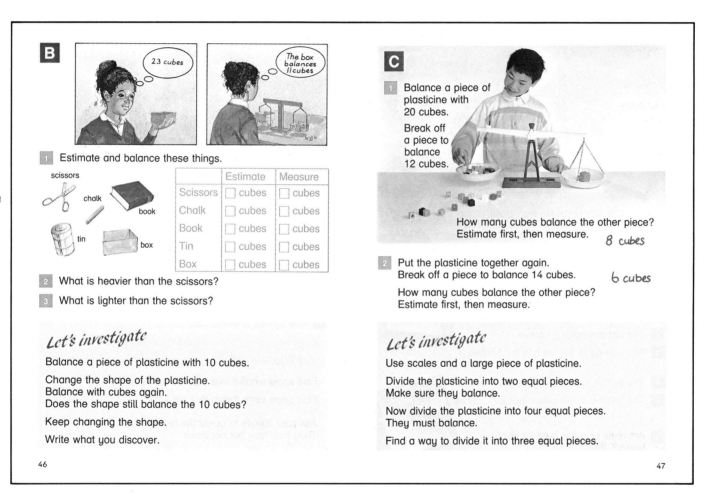

B

1 Estimate and balance these things.

scissors

chalk

book

tin

box

	Estimate	Measure
Scissors	☐ cubes	☐ cubes
Chalk	☐ cubes	☐ cubes
Book	☐ cubes	☐ cubes
Tin	☐ cubes	☐ cubes
Box	☐ cubes	☐ cubes

2 What is heavier than the scissors?

3 What is lighter than the scissors?

Let's investigate

Balance a piece of plasticine with 10 cubes.

Change the shape of the plasticine.
Balance with cubes again.
Does the shape still balance the 10 cubes?

Keep changing the shape.

Write what you discover.

46

C

1 Balance a piece of plasticine with 20 cubes.

Break off a piece to balance 12 cubes.

How many cubes balance the other piece?
Estimate first, then measure.   8 cubes

2 Put the plasticine together again.
Break off a piece to balance 14 cubes.   6 cubes

How many cubes balance the other piece?
Estimate first, then measure.

Let's investigate

Use scales and a large piece of plasticine.

Divide the plasticine into two equal pieces.
Make sure they balance.

Now divide the plasticine into four equal pieces.
They must balance.

Find a way to divide it into three equal pieces.

47

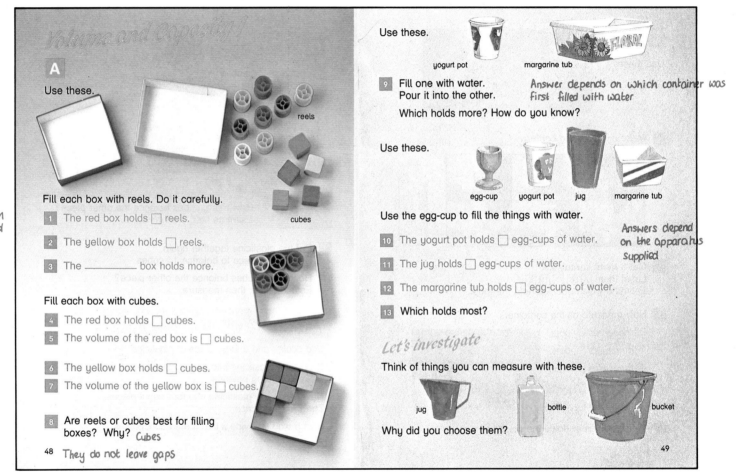

Volume and Capacity 1

A

Use these.

reels

cubes

Answers depend on the boxes supplied

Fill each box with reels. Do it carefully.

1 The red box holds ☐ reels.

2 The yellow box holds ☐ reels.

3 The _____ box holds more.

Fill each box with cubes.

4 The red box holds ☐ cubes.

5 The volume of the red box is ☐ cubes.

6 The yellow box holds ☐ cubes.

7 The volume of the yellow box is ☐ cubes.

8 Are reels or cubes best for filling boxes? Why? *Cubes*

48 *They do not leave gaps*

Use these.

yogurt pot   margarine tub

9 Fill one with water. *Answer depends on which container was*
   Pour it into the other. *first filled with water*

Which holds more? How do you know?

Use these.

egg-cup   yogurt pot   jug   margarine tub

Use the egg-cup to fill the things with water.

Answers depend on the apparatus supplied

10 The yogurt pot holds ☐ egg-cups of water.

11 The jug holds ☐ egg-cups of water.

12 The margarine tub holds ☐ egg-cups of water.

13 Which holds most?

Let's investigate

Think of things you can measure with these.

jug   bottle   bucket

Why did you choose them?

49

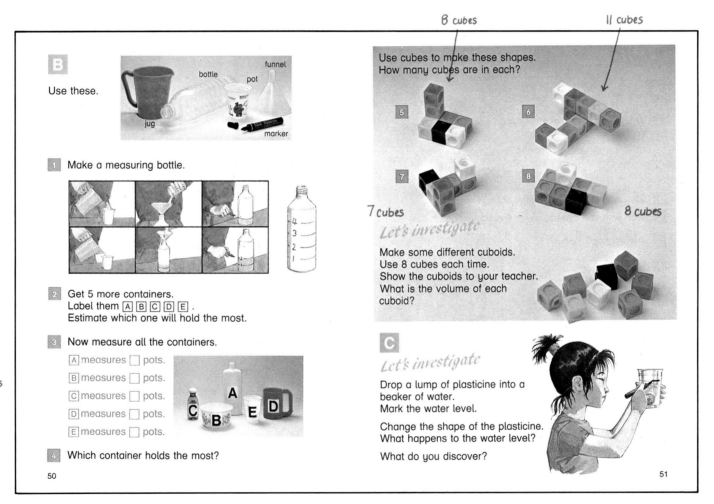

B

Use these.

jug   bottle   pot   funnel   marker

1 Make a measuring bottle.

2 Get 5 more containers.
Label them A B C D E .
Estimate which one will hold the most.

3 Now measure all the containers.

A measures ☐ pots.
B measures ☐ pots.
C measures ☐ pots.
D measures ☐ pots.
E measures ☐ pots.

4 Which container holds the most?

Answers depend on the containers supplied

50

8 cubes   11 cubes

Use cubes to make these shapes.
How many cubes are in each?

5   6

7   8

7 cubes   8 cubes

Let's investigate

Make some different cuboids.
Use 8 cubes each time.
Show the cuboids to your teacher.
What is the volume of each cuboid?

C

Let's investigate

Drop a lump of plasticine into a beaker of water.
Mark the water level.

Change the shape of the plasticine.
What happens to the water level?

What do you discover?

51

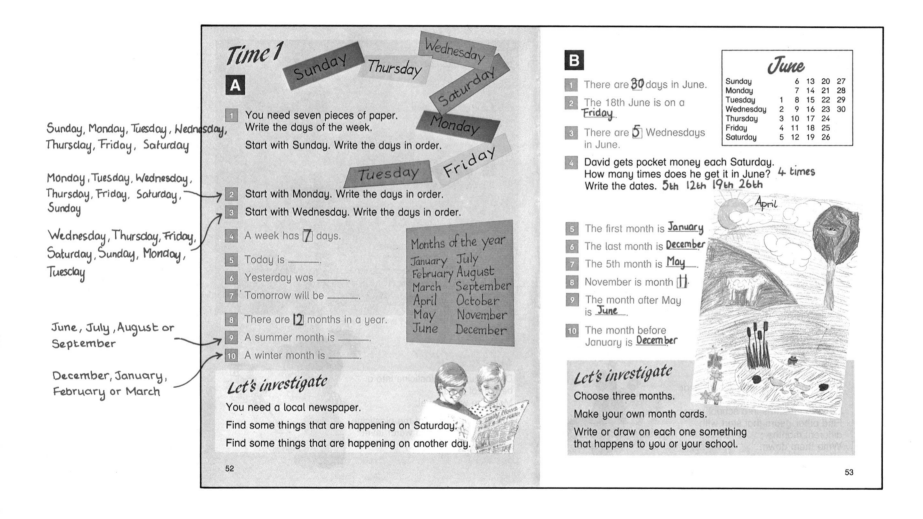

Time 1

A

Sunday   Thursday   Wednesday   Saturday   Monday   Tuesday   Friday

1 You need seven pieces of paper.
Write the days of the week.

Start with Sunday. Write the days in order.

Sunday, Monday, Tuesday, Wednesday, Thursday, Friday, Saturday

2 Start with Monday. Write the days in order.

Monday, Tuesday, Wednesday, Thursday, Friday, Saturday, Sunday

3 Start with Wednesday. Write the days in order.

Wednesday, Thursday, Friday, Saturday, Sunday, Monday, Tuesday

4 A week has 7 days.

5 Today is _____.

6 Yesterday was _____.

7 Tomorrow will be _____.

8 There are 12 months in a year.

9 A summer month is _____.

June, July, August or September

10 A winter month is _____.

December, January, February or March

Months of the year

January	July
February	August
March	September
April	October
May	November
June	December

Let's investigate

You need a local newspaper.

Find some things that are happening on Saturday.

Find some things that are happening on another day.

52

B

1 There are 30 days in June.

2 The 18th June is on a *Friday*.

3 There are 5 Wednesdays in June.

4 David gets pocket money each Saturday. How many times does he get it in June? *4 times*
Write the dates. *5th 12th 19th 26th*

5 The first month is *January*

6 The last month is *December*

7 The 5th month is *May*

8 November is month 11.

9 The month after May is *June*

10 The month before January is *December*

June

Sunday		6	13	20	27
Monday		7	14	21	28
Tuesday	1	8	15	22	29
Wednesday	2	9	16	23	30
Thursday	3	10	17	24	
Friday	4	11	18	25	
Saturday	5	12	19	26	

April

Let's investigate

Choose three months.

Make your own month cards.

Write or draw on each one something that happens to you or your school.

53

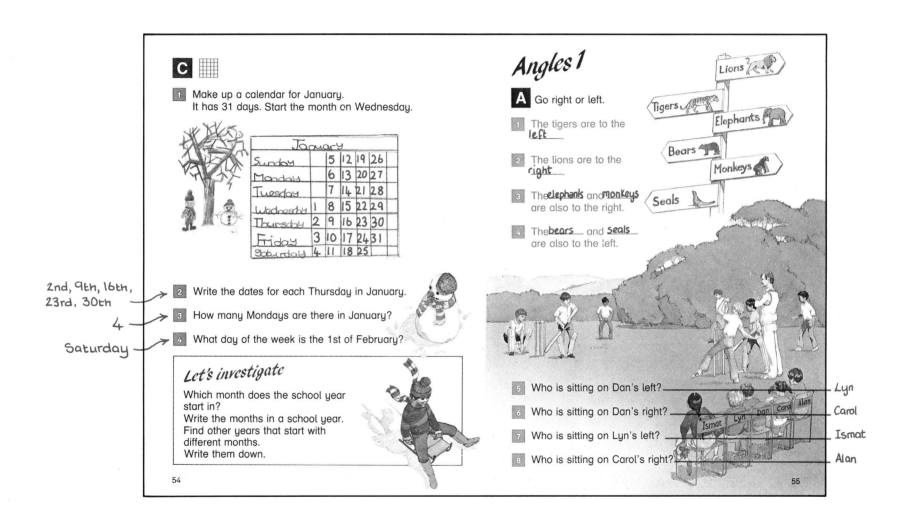

C

1 Make up a calendar for January.
It has 31 days. Start the month on Wednesday.

January				
Sunday	5	12	19	26
Monday	6	13	20	27
Tuesday	7	14	21	28
Wednesday	1	8	15	22	29
Thursday	2	9	16	23	30
Friday	3	10	17	24	31
Saturday	4	11	18	25

2nd, 9th, 16th, 23rd, 30th →

2 Write the dates for each Thursday in January.

4 →

3 How many Mondays are there in January?

Saturday →

4 What day of the week is the 1st of February?

Let's investigate

Which month does the school year start in?
Write the months in a school year.
Find other years that start with different months.
Write them down.

54

Angles 1

A Go right or left.

1 The tigers are to the **left**.

2 The lions are to the **right**.

3 The **elephants** and **monkeys** are also to the right.

4 The **bears** and **seals** are also to the left.

Lions

Tigers

Elephants

Bears

Monkeys

Seals

5 Who is sitting on Dan's left? — Lyn

6 Who is sitting on Dan's right? — Carol

7 Who is sitting on Lyn's left? — Ismat

8 Who is sitting on Carol's right? — Alan

55

Let's investigate

n	c	r	t	g	a	d	o	t

Start at [c]. Right 4. Left 2.

c		a		t

What are these words?

Start at [d]. Right 1. Left 3.

Start at [r]. Right 3. Left 1.

Make up some of your own.

What is the longest word you can make?

B

left   **1** At the post-box turn _____.

right   **2** At the tree turn _____.

right   **3** At the lamp-post turn _____.

right   **4** After the crossing turn _____.

left   **5** At the traffic lights turn _____.

56

Let's investigate

F means **forward**. ↑
R means **right**. →
L means **left**. ←

Write a way to score a goal.

Say how many squares
F, R or L each time.

You can start like this.
F1, R1, F2, L1

Find other ways to score goals.

Goal

Start

C

1 Bashir sits down.
Isobel sits on his right.
Garry is on Bashir's left.
Angie is on Isobel's right.

Write their names in order.

Garry   Bashir   Isobel   Angie

Let's investigate

Draw four faces. Give them names.

Use another piece of paper.
Write sentences like those in question 1.

Show your friends the sentences but not the faces.
Ask your friends to draw the faces and names.

Were they right?

57

Number 6

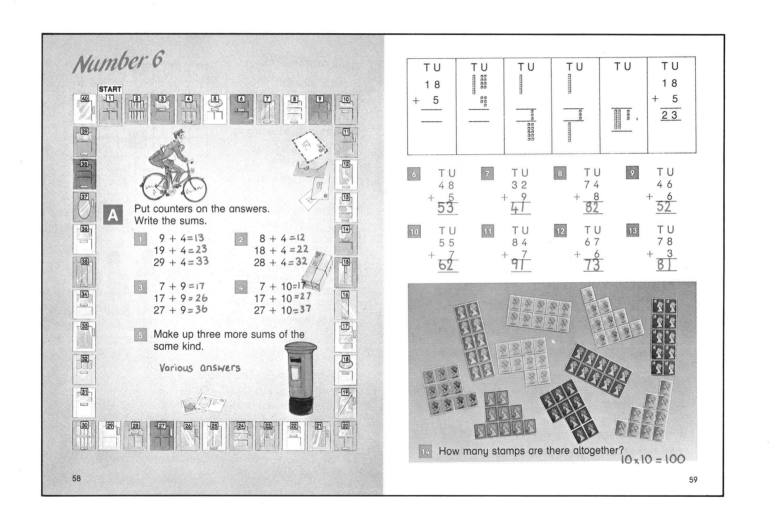

START

A Put counters on the answers.
Write the sums.

1
9 + 4 = 13
19 + 4 = 23
29 + 4 = 33

2
8 + 4 = 12
18 + 4 = 22
28 + 4 = 32

3
7 + 9 = 17
17 + 9 = 26
27 + 9 = 36

4
7 + 10 = 17
17 + 10 = 27
27 + 10 = 37

5 Make up three more sums of the
same kind.

Various answers

58

T U	T U	T U	T U	T U	T U
1 8					1 8
+ 5					+ 5
					2 3

6
T U
4 8
+ 5
53

7
T U
3 2
+ 9
41

8
T U
7 4
+ 8
82

9
T U
4 6
+ 6
52

10
T U
5 5
+ 7
62

11
T U
8 4
+ 7
91

12
T U
6 7
+ 6
73

13
T U
7 8
+ 3
81

14 How many stamps are there altogether?

10 × 10 = 100

59

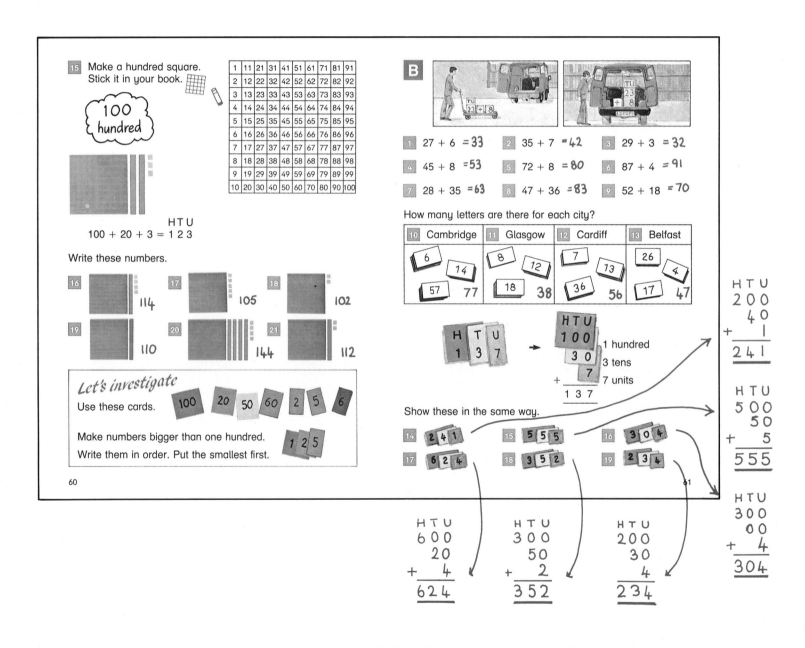

15 Make a hundred square.
Stick it in your book.

1	11	21	31	41	51	61	71	81	91
2	12	22	32	42	52	62	72	82	92
3	13	23	33	43	53	63	73	83	93
4	14	24	34	44	54	64	74	84	94
5	15	25	35	45	55	65	75	85	95
6	16	26	36	46	56	66	76	86	96
7	17	27	37	47	57	67	77	87	97
8	18	28	38	48	58	68	78	88	98
9	19	29	39	49	59	69	79	89	99
10	20	30	40	50	60	70	80	90	100

100 hundred

H T U
100 + 20 + 3 = 1 2 3

Write these numbers.

16 114   **17** 105   **18** 102

19 110   **20** 144   **21** 112

Let's investigate

Use these cards.   100 20 50 60 2 5 6

Make numbers bigger than one hundred.   1 2 5

Write them in order. Put the smallest first.

60

B

1 27 + 6 = 33   **2** 35 + 7 = 42   **3** 29 + 3 = 32

4 45 + 8 = 53   **5** 72 + 8 = 80   **6** 87 + 4 = 91

7 28 + 35 = 63   **8** 47 + 36 = 83   **9** 52 + 18 = 70

How many letters are there for each city?

10 Cambridge	**11** Glasgow	**12** Cardiff	**13** Belfast
6 14 57 **77**	8 12 18 **38**	7 13 36 **56**	26 4 17 **47**

H T U
1 3 7   →   H T U
1 0 0   1 hundred
  3 0   3 tens
+   7   7 units
1 3 7

Show these in the same way.

14 241   **15** 555   **16** 304

17 624   **18** 352   **19** 234

H T U
6 0 0
  2 0
+   4
6 2 4

H T U
3 0 0
  5 0
+   2
3 5 2

H T U
2 0 0
  3 0
+   4
2 3 4

H T U
2 0 0
  4 0
+   1
2 4 1

H T U
5 0 0
  5 0
+   5
5 5 5

H T U
3 0 0
  0 0
+   4
3 0 4

61

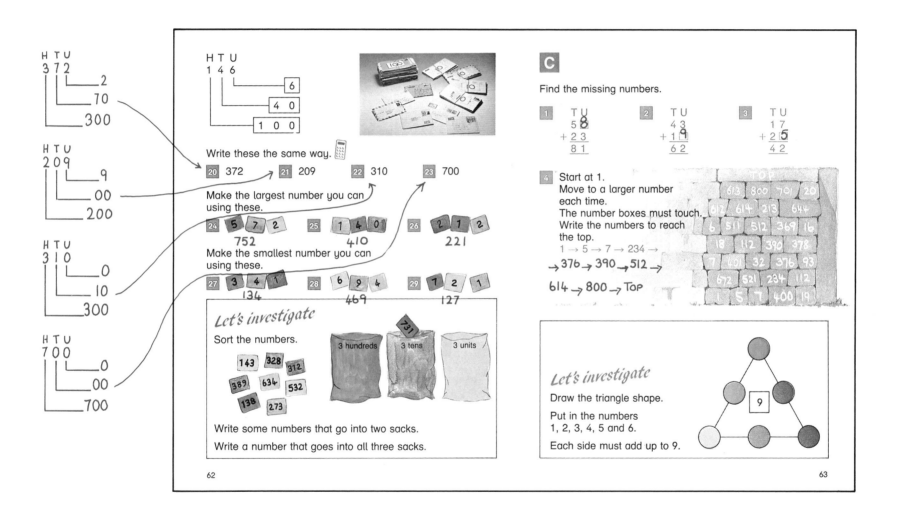

H T U
3 7 2
└── 2
└── 7 0
└── 3 0 0

H T U
2 0 9
└── 9
└── 0 0
└── 2 0 0

H T U
3 1 0
└── 0
└── 1 0
└── 3 0 0

H T U
7 0 0
└── 0
└── 0 0
└── 7 0 0

H T U
1 4 6
└── 6
└── 4 0
└── 1 0 0

Write these the same way.

20 372   21 209   22 310   23 700

Make the largest number you can using these.

24 5 7 2   25 1 4 0   26 2 1 2
    752   410   221

Make the smallest number you can using these.

27 3 4 1   28 6 9 4   29 7 2 1
    134   469   127

Let's investigate

Sort the numbers.

143 328 312 389 634 532 138 273

731

3 hundreds   3 tens   3 units

Write some numbers that go into two sacks.

Write a number that goes into all three sacks.

C

Find the missing numbers.

1   T U   2   T U   3   T U
     5 8   4 3   1 7
   + 2 3   + 1 9   + 2 5
   ─────   ─────   ─────
     8 1   6 2   4 2

4 Start at 1.
   Move to a larger number each time.
   The number boxes must touch.
   Write the numbers to reach the top.

   1 → 5 → 7 → 234 →
   → 376 → 390 → 512 →
   614 → 800 → Top

TOP
613 800 701 20
617 614 213 644
6 511 512 369 16
18 112 390 378
7 401 32 376 93
672 521 234 112
1 5 7 400 19

Let's investigate

Draw the triangle shape.

Put in the numbers 1, 2, 3, 4, 5 and 6.

Each side must add up to 9.

9

62   63

Number 7

A

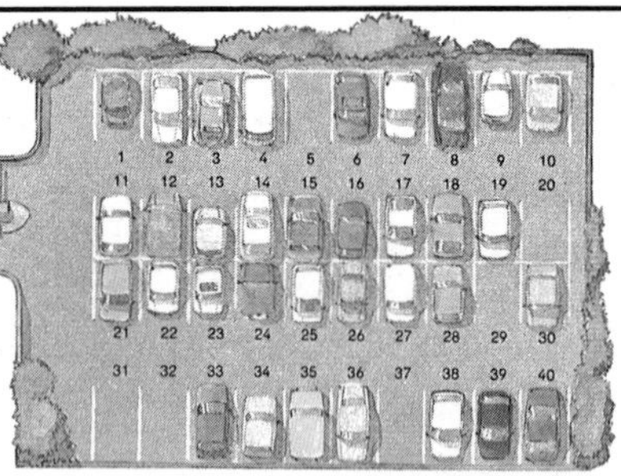

1 If 8 cars go, how many are left?

$34 - 8 = 26$

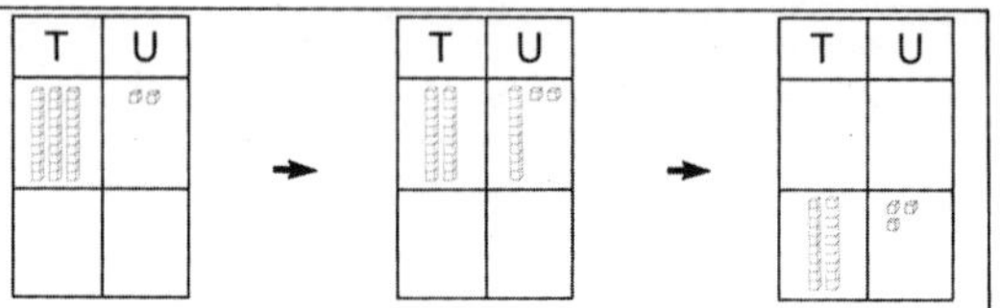

| T | U |
| | |

→

| T | U |
| | |

→

| T | U |
| | |

```
  T U
  3 2
-   9
-----
```

```
  T U
  3 2
-   9
-----
  2 3
```

2
```
  T U
  5 2
-   7
-----
  45
```

3
```
  T U
  5 2
- 1 7
-----
  35
```

4
```
  T U
  5 2
- 2 7
-----
  25
```

5 Look for a pattern. What is the next one?

6
```
  T U
  4 3
-   5
-----
  38
```

7
```
  T U
  4 3
- 1 5
-----
  28
```

8
```
  T U
  4 3
- 2 5
-----
  18
```

(left margin)
```
  T U
  5 2
- 3 7
-----
  1 5
```

64

Write the numbers.

9 H T U   **10** H T U   **11** H T U   **12** H T U

2 5 3   1 3 6   3 2 5   1 0 4

Draw an abacus to show each number.

13 123   **14** 357   **15** 245   **16** 149

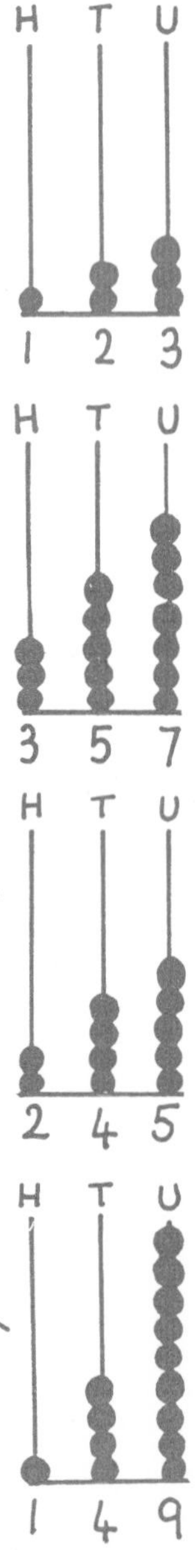

Let's investigate

Make number sentences like this.

$9 - 5 = 4$ $4 + 5 = 9$

```
  9  +
- 5    4
=
```

Choose three other numbers.
Make number sentences.

```
□  -
+  □
=  □
```

Try it with other numbers.

65

(right margin abacus labels)

H T U
1 2 3

H T U
3 5 7

H T U
2 4 5

H T U
1 4 9

Three hundred and seventy five

Four hundred and fifteen

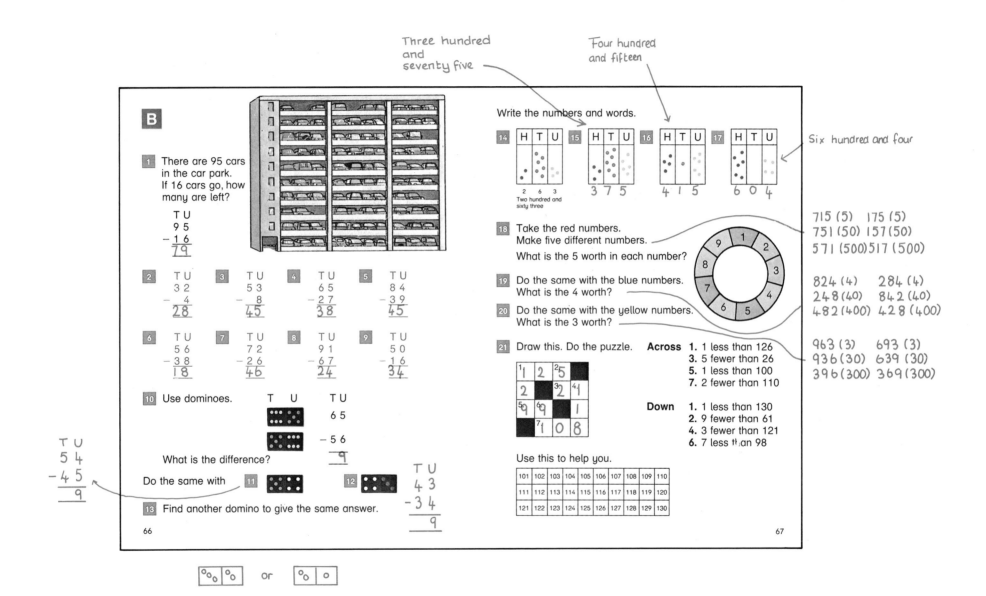

B

1 There are 95 cars in the car park. If 16 cars go, how many are left?

```
  T U
  9 5
- 1 6
───────
  7 9
```

2
```
  T U
  3 2
-   4
─────
  2 8
```

3
```
  T U
  5 3
-   8
─────
  4 5
```

4
```
  T U
  6 5
- 2 7
─────
  3 8
```

5
```
  T U
  8 4
- 3 9
─────
  4 5
```

6
```
  T U
  5 6
- 3 8
─────
  1 8
```

7
```
  T U
  7 2
- 2 6
─────
  4 6
```

8
```
  T U
  9 1
- 6 7
─────
  2 4
```

9
```
  T U
  5 0
- 1 6
─────
  3 4
```

10 Use dominoes.

```
T   U        T U
             6 5

           - 5 6
           ─────
What is the    9
difference?
```

Do the same with **11**   **12**

```
  T U
  4 3
- 3 4
─────
    9
```

13 Find another domino to give the same answer.

```
  T U
  5 4
- 4 5
─────
    9
```

66

Write the numbers and words.

14
```
H T U
```
2 6 3
Two hundred and sixty three

15
```
H T U
```
3 7 5

16
```
H T U
```
4 1 5

17
```
H T U
```
6 0 4

Six hundred and four

18 Take the red numbers. Make five different numbers.

What is the 5 worth in each number?

715 (5)   175 (5)
751 (50) 157 (50)
571 (500) 517 (500)

19 Do the same with the blue numbers. What is the 4 worth?

824 (4)   284 (4)
248 (40) 842 (40)
482 (400) 428 (400)

20 Do the same with the yellow numbers. What is the 3 worth?

963 (3)   693 (3)
936 (30) 639 (30)
396 (300) 369 (300)

21 Draw this. Do the puzzle.

```
┌─┬─┬─┬─┐
│1│2│ │5│
│1│2│ │ │
├─┼─┼─┼─┤
│2│ │3│4│
│2│ │2│1│
├─┼─┼─┼─┤
│5│6│ │ │
│9│9│ │1│
├─┼─┼─┼─┤
│ │7│ │ │
│ │1│0│8│
└─┴─┴─┴─┘
```

Across
1. 1 less than 126
3. 5 fewer than 26
5. 1 less than 100
7. 2 fewer than 110

Down
1. 1 less than 130
2. 9 fewer than 61
4. 3 fewer than 121
6. 7 less than 98

Use this to help you.

101	102	103	104	105	106	107	108	109	110
111	112	113	114	115	116	117	118	119	120
121	122	123	124	125	126	127	128	129	130

67

```
┌──────┬─────┐      ┌─────┬───┐
│ °°₀  │ °°₀ │  or  │ °°  │ ° │
└──────┴─────┘      └─────┴───┘
```

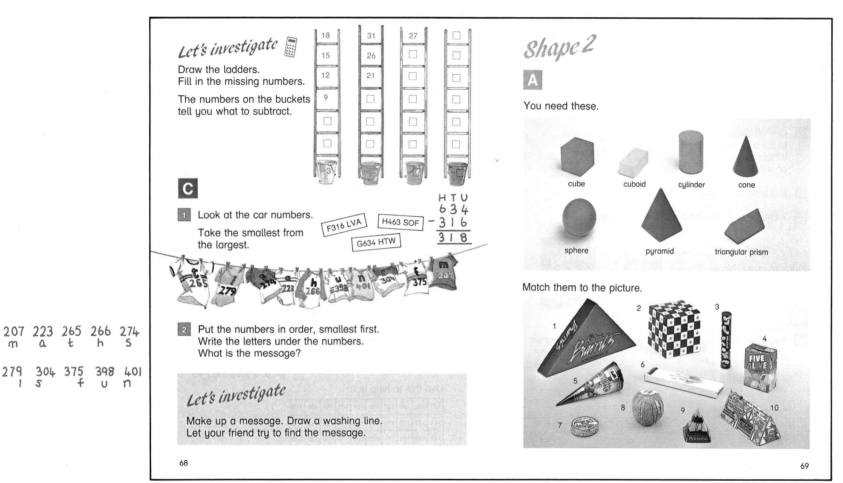

Let's investigate

Draw the ladders.
Fill in the missing numbers.

The numbers on the buckets tell you what to subtract.

C

1 Look at the car numbers.

Take the smallest from the largest.

F316 LVA   H463 SOF

G634 HTW

```
H T U
6 3 4
-3 1 6
  3 1 8
```

2 Put the numbers in order, smallest first.
Write the letters under the numbers.
What is the message?

207 223 265 266 274
 m   a   t   h   s

279 304 375 398 401
 i   s   f   u   n

Let's investigate

Make up a message. Draw a washing line.
Let your friend try to find the message.

68

Shape 2

A

You need these.

cube   cuboid   cylinder   cone

sphere   pyramid   triangular prism

Match them to the picture.

1 Triangular prism
2 Cube
3 Cylinder
4 Cuboid
5 Cone
6 Cuboid
7 Cylinder
8 Sphere
9 Pyramid
10 Triangular prism

69

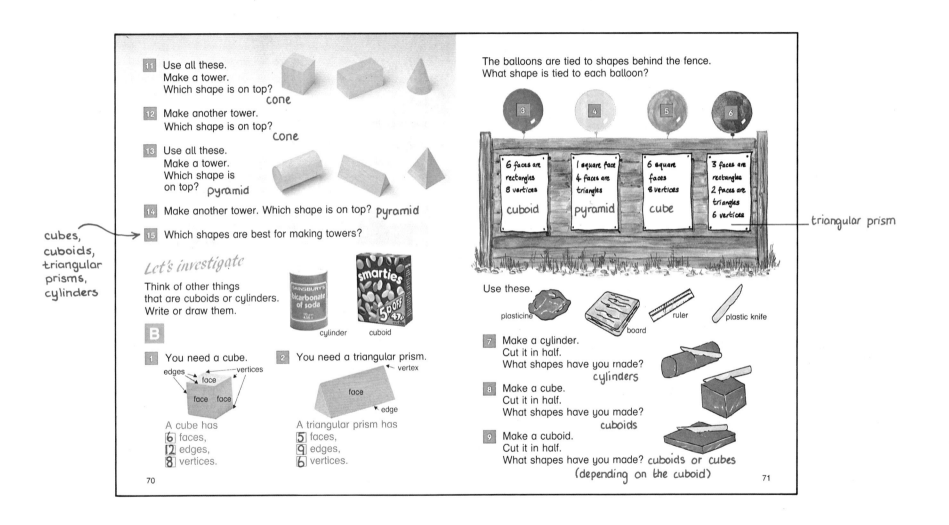

11 Use all these.
Make a tower.
Which shape is on top? **cone**

12 Make another tower.
Which shape is on top? **cone**

13 Use all these.
Make a tower.
Which shape is
on top? **pyramid**

14 Make another tower. Which shape is on top? **pyramid**

15 Which shapes are best for making towers?

cubes, cuboids, triangular prisms, cylinders

Let's investigate

Think of other things
that are cuboids or cylinders.
Write or draw them.

cylinder   cuboid

B

1 You need a cube.

edges   vertices
face
face   face

A cube has
6 faces,
12 edges,
8 vertices.

2 You need a triangular prism.

vertex
face
edge

A triangular prism has
5 faces,
9 edges,
6 vertices.

70

The balloons are tied to shapes behind the fence.
What shape is tied to each balloon?

3   4   5   6

6 faces are
rectangles
8 vertices
cuboid

1 square face
4 faces are
triangles
pyramid

6 square
faces
8 vertices
cube

3 faces are
rectangles
2 faces are
triangles
6 vertices
triangular prism

Use these.

plasticine   board   ruler   plastic knife

7 Make a cylinder.
Cut it in half.
What shapes have you made?
cylinders

8 Make a cube.
Cut it in half.
What shapes have you made?
cuboids

9 Make a cuboid.
Cut it in half.
What shapes have you made? **cuboids or cubes
(depending on the cuboid)**

71

Many books and boxes are cuboids. Cones, cubes and spheres are less common.

The cuboid is (probably) the most popular shape because, for example, it stacks well and saves space.

Let's investigate

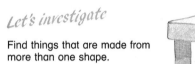

Find things that are made from more than one shape.

Write their shapes, like this.

This table is made from 1 cuboid and 4 cylinders.

C

1 Look for shapes in your classroom.
   Write the names of things you find.

2 Which is the most popular shape?
   Why do you think this is?

Let's investigate

Look at all these shapes.
Put the shapes together in different ways.
Try to make them look like buildings.
Fold some sheets of paper to look like the shapes.

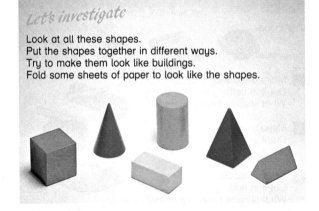

72

Number 8

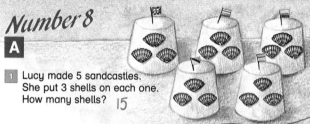

A

1 Lucy made 5 sandcastles.
   She put 3 shells on each one.
   How many shells? *15*

2 Copy the pattern of 3.
   Go as far as 30.

3 Now make the pattern of 4
   as far as 40.

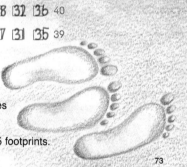

Use your patterns to fill in the numbers.

4 3 6 9 *12* *15* *18* 21 *24* *27* 30

5 1 4 7 *10* *13* *16* *19* *22* *25* 28

6 4 8 12 *16* *20* *24* 28 *32* *36* 40

7 3 7 11 *15* *19* 23 27 *31* *35* 39

8 1 footprint → 5 toes
   $1 \times 5 = 5$

   2 footprints → 5 + 5 toes
   $2 \times 5 = 10$

   Write the pattern up to 5 footprints.

73

1	2	3
4	5	6
7	8	9
10	11	12
13	14	15
16	17	18
19	20	21
22	23	24
25	26	27
28	29	30

1	2	3	4
5	6	7	8
9	10	11	12
13	14	15	16
17	18	19	20
21	22	23	24
25	26	27	28
29	30	31	32
33	34	35	36
37	38	39	40

3 footprints → 5 + 5 + 5 toes $3 \times 5 = 15$

4 footprints → 5 + 5 + 5 + 5 toes $4 \times 5 = 20$

5 footprints → 5 + 5 + 5 + 5 + 5 toes $5 \times 5 = 25$

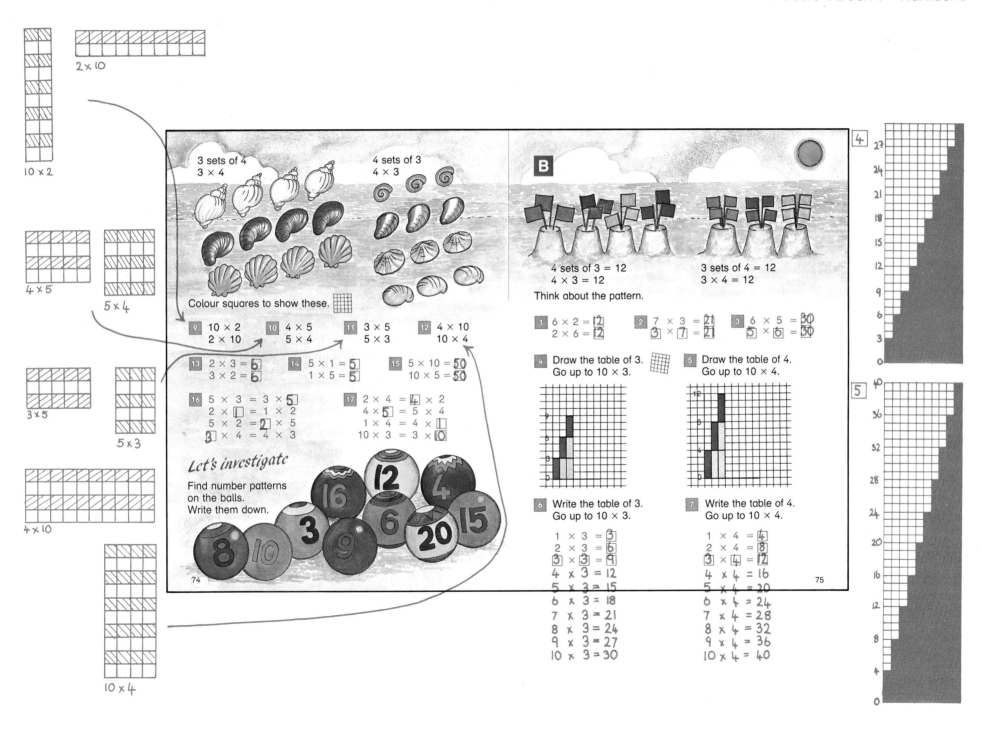

2 × 10

10 × 2

4 × 5

5 × 4

3 × 5

5 × 3

4 × 10

10 × 4

3 sets of 4
3 × 4

4 sets of 3
4 × 3

Colour squares to show these. ▦

9 10 × 2
2 × 10

10 4 × 5
5 × 4

11 3 × 5
5 × 3

12 4 × 10
10 × 4

13 2 × 3 = 6
3 × 2 = 6

14 5 × 1 = 5
1 × 5 = 5

15 5 × 10 = 50
10 × 5 = 50

16 5 × 3 = 3 × 5
2 × 1 = 1 × 2
5 × 2 = 2 × 5
3 × 4 = 4 × 3

17 2 × 4 = 4 × 2
4 × 5 = 5 × 4
1 × 4 = 4 × 1
10 × 3 = 3 × 10

Let's investigate

Find number patterns
on the balls.
Write them down.

74

B

4 sets of 3 = 12
4 × 3 = 12

3 sets of 4 = 12
3 × 4 = 12

Think about the pattern.

1 6 × 2 = 12
2 × 6 = 12

2 7 × 3 = 21
3 × 7 = 21

3 6 × 5 = 30
5 × 6 = 30

4 Draw the table of 3.
Go up to 10 × 3. ▦

5 Draw the table of 4.
Go up to 10 × 4.

6 Write the table of 3.
Go up to 10 × 3.

1 × 3 = 3
2 × 3 = 6
3 × 3 = 9
4 × 3 = 12
5 × 3 = 15
6 × 3 = 18
7 × 3 = 21
8 × 3 = 24
9 × 3 = 27
10 × 3 = 30

7 Write the table of 4.
Go up to 10 × 4.

1 × 4 = 4
2 × 4 = 8
3 × 4 = 12
4 × 4 = 16
5 × 4 = 20
6 × 4 = 24
7 × 4 = 28
8 × 4 = 32
9 × 4 = 36
10 × 4 = 40

75

4

27
24
21
18
15
12
9
6
3
0

5

40
36
32
28
24
20
16
12
8
4
0

8 How many children in 7 boats? **21**
9 How many children in 8 boats? **24**

3 children
in each boat

Time yourself

10 2 × 3 = **6**   11 8 × 3 = **24**   12 5 × 3 = **15**

13 4 × 3 = **12**   14 10 × 3 = **30**   15 6 × 3 = **18**

16 1 × 1 = **1**   17 3 × 3 = **9**   18 10 × 10 = **100**

19 2 × 2 = **4**   20 5 × 5 = **25**   21 4 × 4 = **16**

Let's investigate

This 100 square shows
the pattern of 2.

Use 100 squares.
Try the pattern of 3
and the pattern of 4.

Find one more pattern.

1	2	3	4	5	6	7	8	9	10
11	12	13	14	15	16	17	18	19	20
21	22	23	24	25	26	27	28	29	30
31	32	33	34	35	36	37	38	39	40
41	42	43	44	45	46	47	48	49	50
51	52	53	54	55	56	57	58	59	60
61	62	63	64	65	66	67	68	69	70
71	72	73	74	75	76	77	78	79	80
81	82	83	84	85	86	87	88	89	90
91	92	93	94	95	96	97	98	99	100

76

C

1 An octopus has 8 legs.
How many legs do 4 octopuses have?   **32**

2 A crab has 2 big claws.
How many big claws do 8 crabs have?   **16**

3 A starfish has 5 arms.
How many arms do 10 starfish have?   **50**

4 This fish has 7 fins.
How many fins do 3 fish have?   **21**

5 A fish has 2 eyes.
How many eyes do 7 fish have?   **14**

6 The tide comes in twice each day.
How many times does it come in during a week?   **14**

Let's investigate

Use the numbers to make up
as many multiplications as you can.

□ × □ = □

You may use the same number
more than once.

Write the answer each time.

2 =

5 × 10

3 4

77

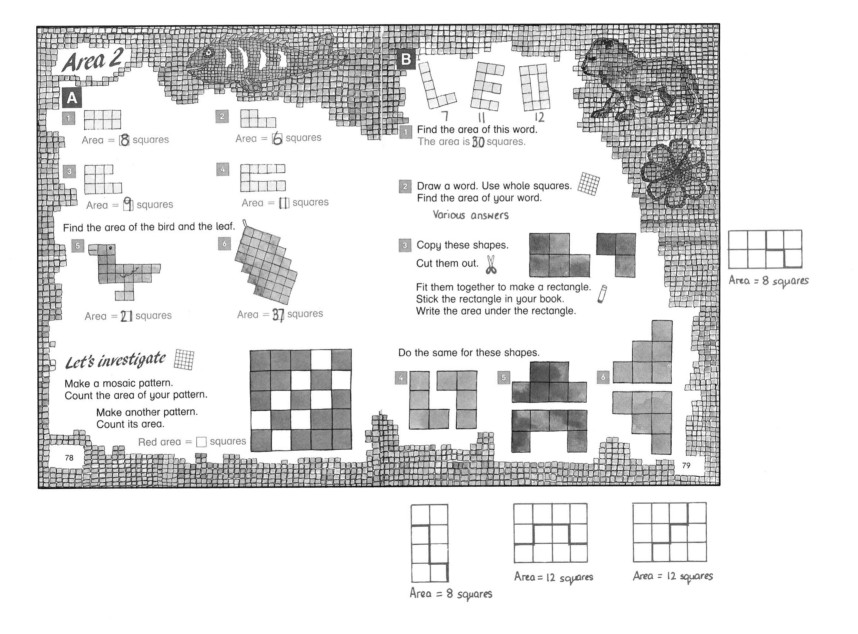

Area 2

A

1. Area = 8 squares

2. Area = 6 squares

3. Area = 9 squares

4. Area = 11 squares

Find the area of the bird and the leaf.

5. Area = 21 squares

6. Area = 37 squares

Let's investigate

Make a mosaic pattern.
Count the area of your pattern.

Make another pattern.
Count its area.

Red area = ☐ squares

B

LEO
7   11   12

1. Find the area of this word.
The area is 30 squares.

2. Draw a word. Use whole squares.
Find the area of your word.

Various answers

3. Copy these shapes.

Cut them out. ✂

Fit them together to make a rectangle.
Stick the rectangle in your book.
Write the area under the rectangle.

Area = 8 squares

Do the same for these shapes.

4.

5.

6.

Area = 8 squares

Area = 12 squares

Area = 12 squares

78

79

Let's investigate

Draw some squares and rectangles.
The area of each shape must be
12 squares or less.

Area = 6 squares

How many shapes can you find?

C

A   B   C   D   E

1 Can you see a pattern?
   What is it?   *Sides increase by one square each time*

2 Draw the next two squares in the pattern.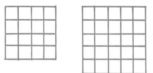

3 Write the area of each square.

Let's investigate

Make a rectangle and a square
each with an area of 4 squares.
Draw your shapes.

Make a larger square.
Make a rectangle with the same area.

Make other squares and rectangles which have
the same area as each other.

80

*1 square, 4 squares,
9 squares, 16 squares.
25 squares*

MODULE FOUR
Book 2
Answers

Notes on all the 'Let's investigate' sections
will be found in the Teacher's Resource Book.

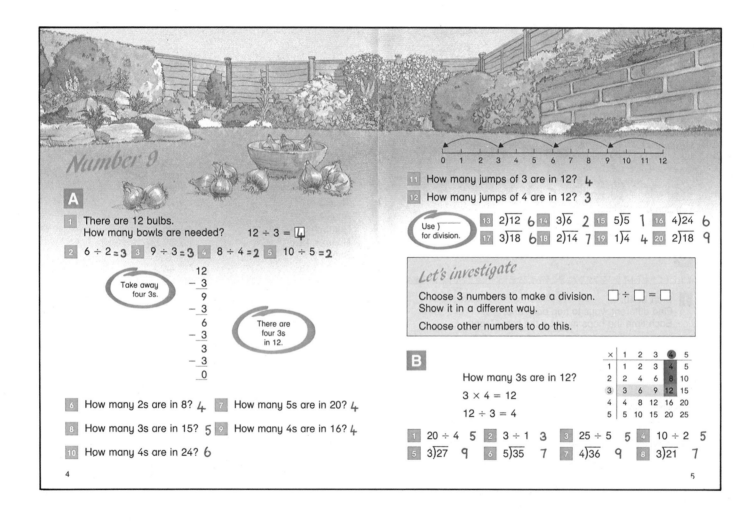

Number 9

A

1. There are 12 bulbs.
   How many bowls are needed? $12 \div 3 = 4$

2. $6 \div 2 = 3$ 3. $9 \div 3 = 3$ 4. $8 \div 4 = 2$ 5. $10 \div 5 = 2$

Take away four 3s.

There are four 3s in 12.

$$\begin{array}{r} 12 \\ -\ 3 \\ \hline 9 \\ -\ 3 \\ \hline 6 \\ -\ 3 \\ \hline 3 \\ -\ 3 \\ \hline 0 \end{array}$$

6. How many 2s are in 8? 4   7. How many 5s are in 20? 4

8. How many 3s are in 15? 5   9. How many 4s are in 16? 4

10. How many 4s are in 24? 6

11. How many jumps of 3 are in 12? 4
12. How many jumps of 4 are in 12? 3

Use) for division.

13. $2\overline{)12}$ 6 14. $3\overline{)6}$ 2 15. $5\overline{)5}$ 1 16. $4\overline{)24}$ 6
17. $3\overline{)18}$ 6 18. $2\overline{)14}$ 7 19. $1\overline{)4}$ 4 20. $2\overline{)18}$ 9

Let's investigate

Choose 3 numbers to make a division. $\square \div \square = \square$
Show it in a different way.

Choose other numbers to do this.

B

How many 3s are in 12?

$3 \times 4 = 12$

$12 \div 3 = 4$

×	1	2	3	4	5
1	1	2	3	4	5
2	2	4	6	8	10
3	3	6	9	12	15
4	4	8	12	16	20
5	5	10	15	20	25

1. $20 \div 4$ 5 2. $3 \div 1$ 3 3. $25 \div 5$ 5 4. $10 \div 2$ 5
5. $3\overline{)27}$ 9 6. $5\overline{)35}$ 7 7. $4\overline{)36}$ 9 8. $3\overline{)21}$ 7

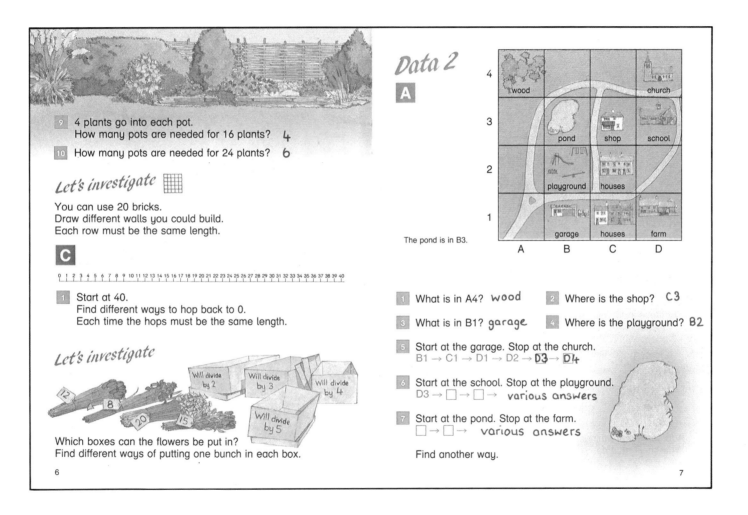

9 4 plants go into each pot.
How many pots are needed for 16 plants?   4

10 How many pots are needed for 24 plants?   6

Let's investigate

You can use 20 bricks.
Draw different walls you could build.
Each row must be the same length.

C

0 1 2 3 4 5 6 7 8 9 10 11 12 13 14 15 16 17 18 19 20 21 22 23 24 25 26 27 28 29 30 31 32 33 34 35 36 37 38 39 40

1 Start at 40.
Find different ways to hop back to 0.
Each time the hops must be the same length.

Hops of 1, 2, 4, 5, 8, 10, 20, 40

Let's investigate

Will divide by 2
Will divide by 3
Will divide by 4
Will divide by 5

Which boxes can the flowers be put in?
Find different ways of putting one bunch in each box.

6

Data 2

A

The pond is in B3.

1 What is in A4? wood   **2** Where is the shop? C3

3 What is in B1? garage   **4** Where is the playground? B2

5 Start at the garage. Stop at the church.
B1 → C1 → D1 → D2 → **D3** → **D4**

6 Start at the school. Stop at the playground.
D3 → ☐ → ☐ →   various answers

7 Start at the pond. Stop at the farm.
☐ → ☐ →   various answers

Find another way.

7

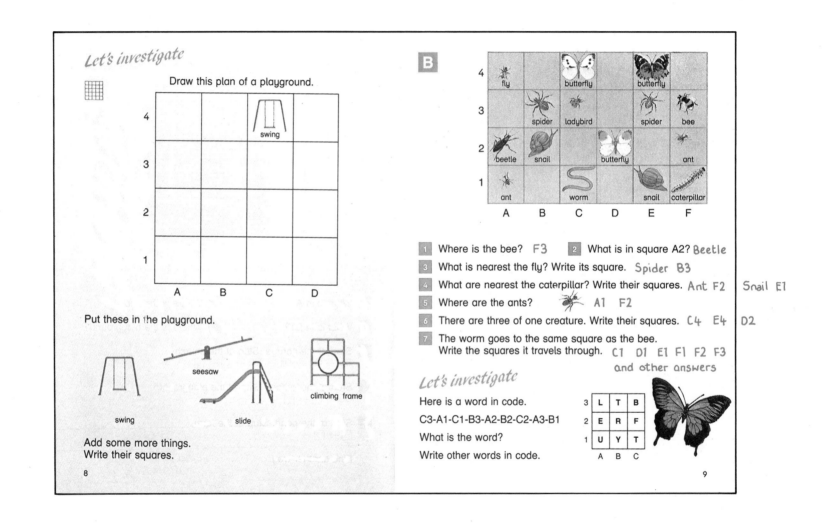

Let's investigate

Draw this plan of a playground.

(grid with axes A, B, C, D across and 1, 2, 3, 4 up; swing drawn in square C4)

Put these in the playground.

swing   seesaw   slide   climbing frame

Add some more things.
Write their squares.

8

B

(grid of insects with axes A–F across and 1–4 up)

	A	B	C	D	E	F
4	fly	butterfly			butterfly	
3		spider	ladybird		spider	bee
2	beetle	snail		butterfly		ant
1	ant	worm			snail	caterpillar

1 Where is the bee? F3   2 What is in square A2? Beetle

3 What is nearest the fly? Write its square. Spider B3

4 What are nearest the caterpillar? Write their squares. Ant F2   Snail E1

5 Where are the ants?   A1 F2

6 There are three of one creature. Write their squares. C4 E4   D2

7 The worm goes to the same square as the bee.
   Write the squares it travels through. C1 D1 E1 F1 F2 F3
   and other answers

Let's investigate

Here is a word in code.

C3-A1-C1-B3-A2-B2-C2-A3-B1

What is the word?

Write other words in code.

	A	B	C
3	L	T	B
2	E	R	F
1	U	Y	T

9

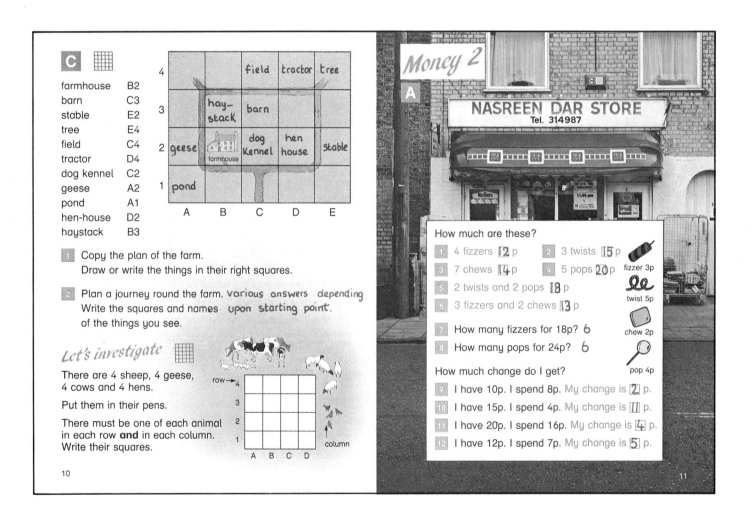

C

farmhouse	B2
barn	C3
stable	E2
tree	E4
field	C4
tractor	D4
dog kennel	C2
geese	A2
pond	A1
hen-house	D2
haystack	B3

Farm plan grid:

	A	B	C	D	E
4			field	tractor	tree
3		hay-stack	barn		
2	geese	farmhouse	dog Kennel	hen house	stable
1	pond				

1 Copy the plan of the farm.
Draw or write the things in their right squares.

2 Plan a journey round the farm. *various answers depending*
Write the squares and names *upon starting point.*
of the things you see.

Let's investigate

There are 4 sheep, 4 geese, 4 cows and 4 hens.

Put them in their pens.

There must be one of each animal in each row **and** in each column.
Write their squares.

row → 4
3
2
1
A B C D
column

10

Money 2

A

NASREEN DAR STORE
Tel. 314987

How much are these?

1 4 fizzers **12** p   **2** 3 twists **15** p   fizzer 3p

3 7 chews **14** p   **4** 5 pops **20** p

5 2 twists and 2 pops **18** p   twist 5p

6 3 fizzers and 2 chews **13** p

7 How many fizzers for 18p? **6**   chew 2p

8 How many pops for 24p? **6**

How much change do I get?   pop 4p

9 I have 10p. I spend 8p. My change is **2** p.

10 I have 15p. I spend 4p. My change is **11** p.

11 I have 20p. I spend 16p. My change is **4** p.

12 I have 12p. I spend 7p. My change is **5** p.

11

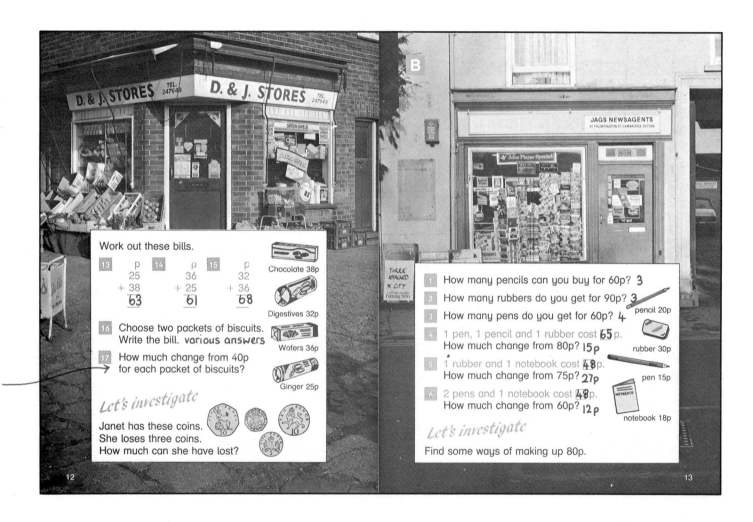

Chocolate 2p
Digestives 8p
Wafers   4p
Ginger   15p

Work out these bills.

13	p	14	p	15	p
	25		36		32
+	38	+	25	+	36
	63		61		68

Chocolate 38p

Digestives 32p

16 Choose two packets of biscuits.
Write the bill. various answers

Wafers 36p

17 How much change from 40p
for each packet of biscuits?

Ginger 25p

Let's investigate

Janet has these coins.
She loses three coins.
How much can she have lost?

1 How many pencils can you buy for 60p? 3
2 How many rubbers do you get for 90p? 3
3 How many pens do you get for 60p? 4

pencil 20p

4 1 pen, 1 pencil and 1 rubber cost 65p.
How much change from 80p? 15p

rubber 30p

5 1 rubber and 1 notebook cost 48p.
How much change from 75p? 27p

pen 15p

6 2 pens and 1 notebook cost 48p.
How much change from 60p? 12p

notebook 18p

Let's investigate

Find some ways of making up 80p.

12

13

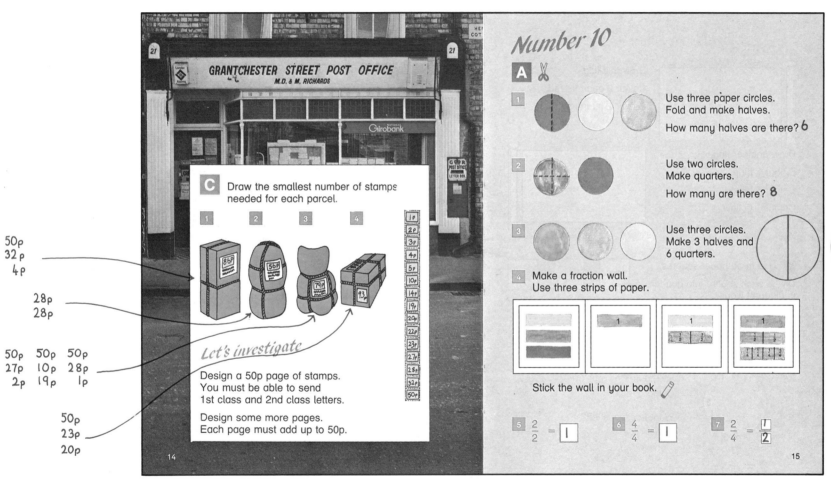

C Draw the smallest number of stamps needed for each parcel.

50p
32p
4p

28p
28p

50p 50p 50p
27p 10p 28p
2p   19p 1p

50p
23p
20p

Let's investigate

Design a 50p page of stamps.
You must be able to send
1st class and 2nd class letters.

Design some more pages.
Each page must add up to 50p.

14

Number 10

A ✂

1 Use three paper circles.
Fold and make halves.
How many halves are there? **6**

2 Use two circles.
Make quarters.
How many are there? **8**

3 Use three circles.
Make 3 halves and
6 quarters.

4 Make a fraction wall.
Use three strips of paper.

Stick the wall in your book. ✏

5 $\frac{2}{2}$ = $\boxed{1}$ 6 $\frac{4}{4}$ = $\boxed{1}$ 7 $\frac{2}{4}$ = $\frac{\boxed{1}}{\boxed{2}}$

15

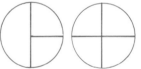

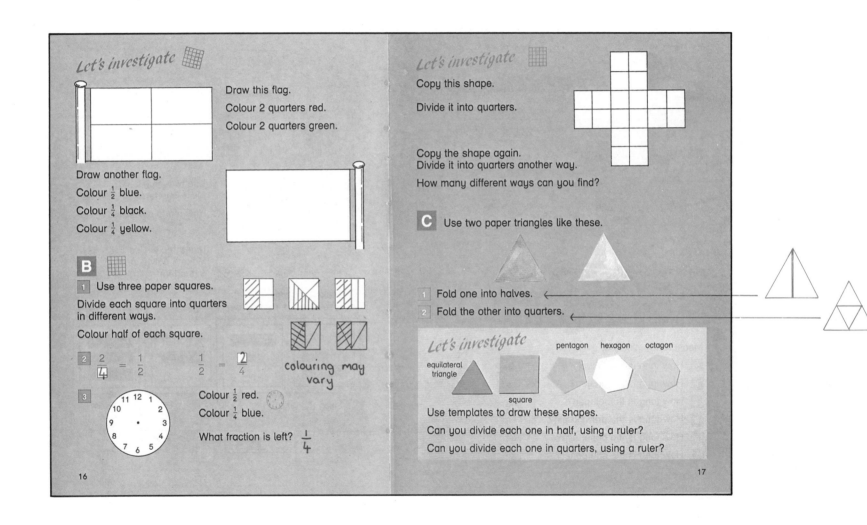

Let's investigate

Draw this flag.

Colour 2 quarters red.

Colour 2 quarters green.

Draw another flag.

Colour $\frac{1}{2}$ blue.

Colour $\frac{1}{4}$ black.

Colour $\frac{1}{4}$ yellow.

B

1 Use three paper squares.

Divide each square into quarters in different ways.

Colour half of each square.

2 $\frac{2}{4} = \frac{1}{2}$ $\frac{1}{2} = \frac{2}{4}$

colouring may vary

3 Colour $\frac{1}{2}$ red.

Colour $\frac{1}{4}$ blue.

What fraction is left? $\frac{1}{4}$

Let's investigate

Copy this shape.

Divide it into quarters.

Copy the shape again.
Divide it into quarters another way.

How many different ways can you find?

C Use two paper triangles like these.

1 Fold one into halves.

2 Fold the other into quarters.

Let's investigate

equilateral triangle   square   pentagon   hexagon   octagon

Use templates to draw these shapes.

Can you divide each one in half, using a ruler?

Can you divide each one in quarters, using a ruler?

16   17

Length 2

A

cm means centimetres.

A ruler measures in centimetres.

1. How long is your ruler? ☐ cm

Rubber

Paper clip

Pencil sharpener

Felt pen

Drawing pin

Crayon

Measure the pictures.

2. How long is the rubber? 5 cm
3. How long is the crayon? 8 cm
4. How long is the felt pen? 9 cm
5. How long is the drawing pin? 1 cm
6. How long is the paper clip? 3 cm
7. How long is the sharpener? 4 cm

18

8. Use your ruler.
Draw a line 5 cm long.

1 2 3 4 5

9. Copy these lines. Write how long they are.

3cm   6cm

9cm

12cm

Estimate and measure the fish.

10. Estimate ☐ cm Measure 5 cm

11. 7cm

12. 10cm

13. 8cm

15. 11cm

14.

16.

9cm

6cm

Use string. Measure the seaweed like this.

The seaweed measures ☐ cm.

Let's investigate

Choose one of the fish. Draw it twice as big.

19

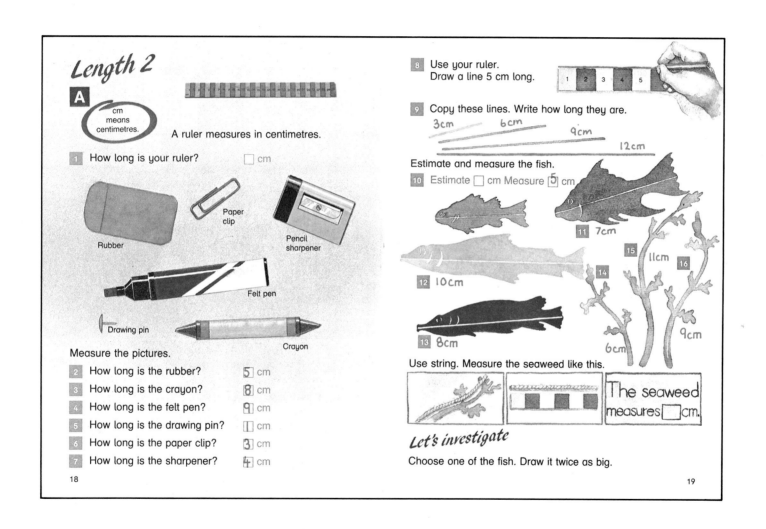

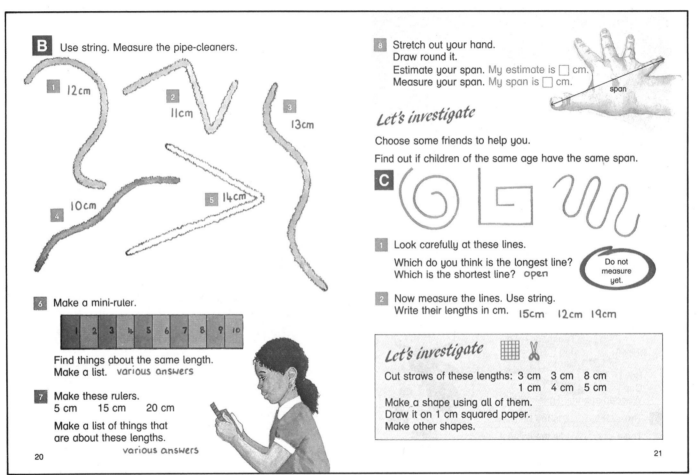

B Use string. Measure the pipe-cleaners.

1 12 cm

2 11 cm

3 13 cm

4 10 cm

5 14 cm

6 Make a mini-ruler.

| 1 | 2 | 3 | 4 | 5 | 6 | 7 | 8 | 9 | 10 |

Find things about the same length.
Make a list. various answers

7 Make these rulers.
5 cm   15 cm   20 cm

Make a list of things that
are about these lengths.
various answers

20

8 Stretch out your hand.
Draw round it.
Estimate your span. My estimate is ☐ cm.
Measure your span. My span is ☐ cm.

span

various answers

Let's investigate

Choose some friends to help you.

Find out if children of the same age have the same span.

C

1 Look carefully at these lines.

Which do you think is the longest line?
Which is the shortest line? open

Do not
measure
yet.

2 Now measure the lines. Use string.
Write their lengths in cm. 15 cm   12 cm   19 cm

Let's investigate

Cut straws of these lengths: 3 cm   3 cm   8 cm
                             1 cm   4 cm   5 cm

Make a shape using all of them.
Draw it on 1 cm squared paper.
Make other shapes.

21

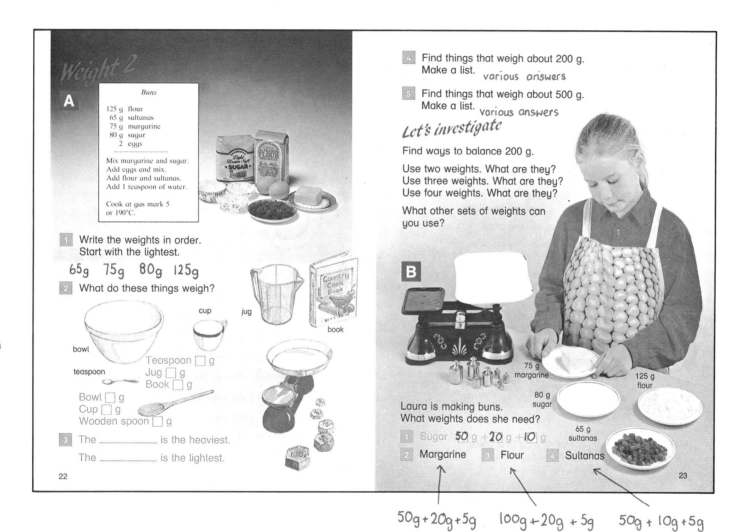

Weight 2

A

Buns

125 g flour
65 g sultanas
75 g margarine
80 g sugar
2 eggs

Mix margarine and sugar.
Add eggs and mix.
Add flour and sultanas.
Add 1 teaspoon of water.

Cook at gas mark 5
or 190°C.

1 Write the weights in order.
Start with the lightest.

65g   75g   80g   125g

2 What do these things weigh?

answers depend on
the apparatus
supplied

bowl
cup
jug
book
teaspoon

Teaspoon ☐ g
Jug ☐ g
Book ☐ g
Bowl ☐ g
Cup ☐ g
Wooden spoon ☐ g

3 The _____ is the heaviest.

The _____ is the lightest.

22

4 Find things that weigh about 200 g.
Make a list. various answers

5 Find things that weigh about 500 g.
Make a list. various answers

Let's investigate

Find ways to balance 200 g.

Use two weights. What are they?
Use three weights. What are they?
Use four weights. What are they?

What other sets of weights can
you use?

B

75 g
margarine

80 g
sugar

125 g
flour

65 g
sultanas

Laura is making buns.
What weights does she need?

1 Sugar **50** g + **20** g + **10** g

2 Margarine   3 Flour   4 Sultanas

50g + 20g + 5g   100g + 20g + 5g   50g + 10g + 5g

23

5   Make weights of 50 g and 200 g.
Use these things.
Label your weights.

Let's investigate

Use your 50 g and 200 g weights.
Find a way to make a 150 g lump of plasticine.

Can you find a way to make a 100 g lump?

Find how to make other weights of plasticine.

C   What do these lunches weigh?

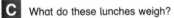

1 565g   2 365g   3 515g

Lunch weights	
2 Sandwiches	90 g
Crisps	25 g
Drink	350 g
Apple	150 g
Banana	125 g
Orange	200 g
Cake	50 g
Chocolate	25 g

4   Which lunch is heaviest? ☐

Let's investigate

Use the chart above.
Make different lunch packs that weigh the same.
You may use some things more than once.

24

Volume and Capacity 2

A

1   Pour water from a litre bottle into a cup.

1 litre fills ☐ cups. ⟵   *answers depend on the apparatus supplied*

2   Pour cups of water into a litre measure.

☐ cups fill the litre measure. *the same as the answer to* ☐

3   ☐ cups fill a ½ litre measure. *half the answer to* ☐

4   Think of ways of using water.
Write down as many as you can. *various answers*

5   Does a paint pot hold more or less than 1 litre?

usually less

25

answers depend on the
apparatus supplied

6 Which hold less than 1 litre?

Which hold more than 1 litre?

Which hold less than $\frac{1}{2}$ litre?

mug   cup   jug   teapot   kettle

Let's investigate

When do you use more than 1 litre of water at home?

Draw or write your answers.

B How many of each
   fill the litre measure?
   answers depend on the
   apparatus supplied

   Estimate, then measure.

1 Pot   estimate ☐
          measure ☐

2 Mug   estimate ☐
          measure ☐

3 Jug   estimate ☐
          measure ☐

4 How many litres fill the bucket?

bucket

mug

yogurt
pot

litre
measure

jug

26

5 The water bottle holds 4 litres.
   The jug holds $\frac{1}{2}$ litre.

   How many jugs can be filled? 8

Let's investigate

Find some containers which hold 1 litre.
They must be different shapes.

Write a sentence about the shape of a litre.

C *Let's investigate*

A mug holds about $\frac{1}{4}$ litre.

How much do you drink with your meals?

How much do you drink in one day?

Estimate how many litres you drink in one
week.

How many litres do your friends drink?

27

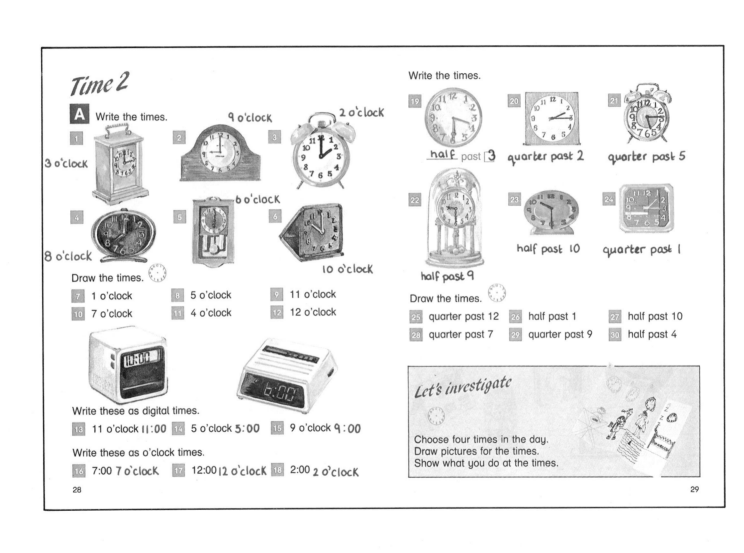

Time 2

A Write the times.

1 — 3 o'clock

2 — 9 o'clock

3 — 2 o'clock

4 — 8 o'clock

5 — 6 o'clock

6 — 10 o'clock

Draw the times.

7 1 o'clock
8 5 o'clock
9 11 o'clock
10 7 o'clock
11 4 o'clock
12 12 o'clock

Write these as digital times.

13 11 o'clock **11:00**   14 5 o'clock **5:00**   15 9 o'clock **9:00**

Write these as o'clock times.

16 7:00 **7 o'clock**   17 12:00 **12 o'clock**   18 2:00 **2 o'clock**

28

Write the times.

19 **half** past **3**
20 quarter past 2
21 quarter past 5

22 half past 9
23 half past 10
24 quarter past 1

Draw the times.

25 quarter past 12   26 half past 1   27 half past 10
28 quarter past 7   29 quarter past 9   30 half past 4

Let's investigate

Choose four times in the day.
Draw pictures for the times.
Show what you do at the times.

29

7
8
9
10
11
12

25
26
27
28
29
30

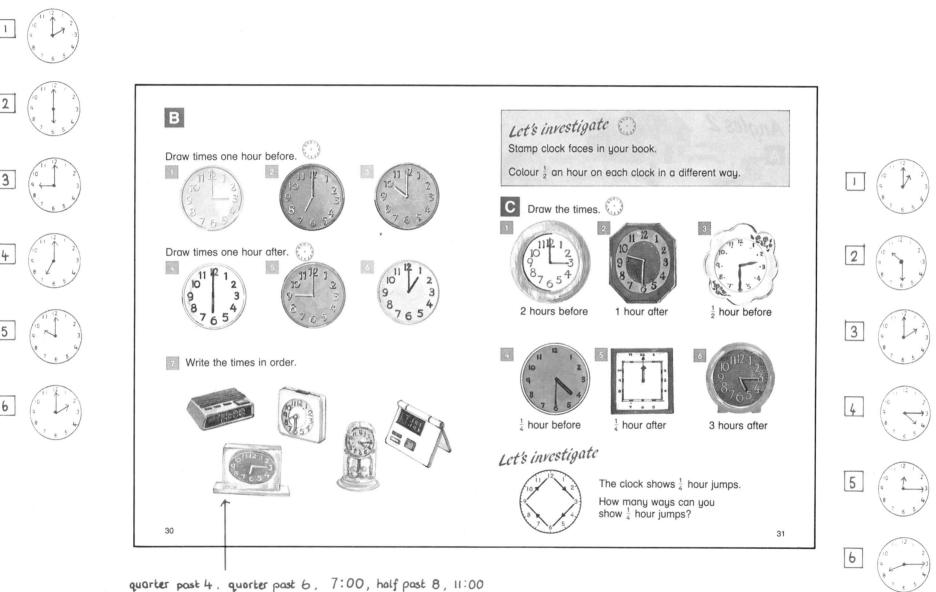

B

Draw times one hour before.

Draw times one hour after.

7 Write the times in order.

quarter past 4 , quarter past 6 , 7:00 , half past 8 , 11:00
(answers may be written in any form)

Let's investigate

Stamp clock faces in your book.

Colour $\frac{1}{2}$ an hour on each clock in a different way.

C Draw the times.

2 hours before   1 hour after $\frac{1}{2}$ hour before

$\frac{1}{4}$ hour before $\frac{1}{4}$ hour after   3 hours after

Let's investigate

The clock shows $\frac{1}{4}$ hour jumps.

How many ways can you show $\frac{1}{4}$ hour jumps?

30

31

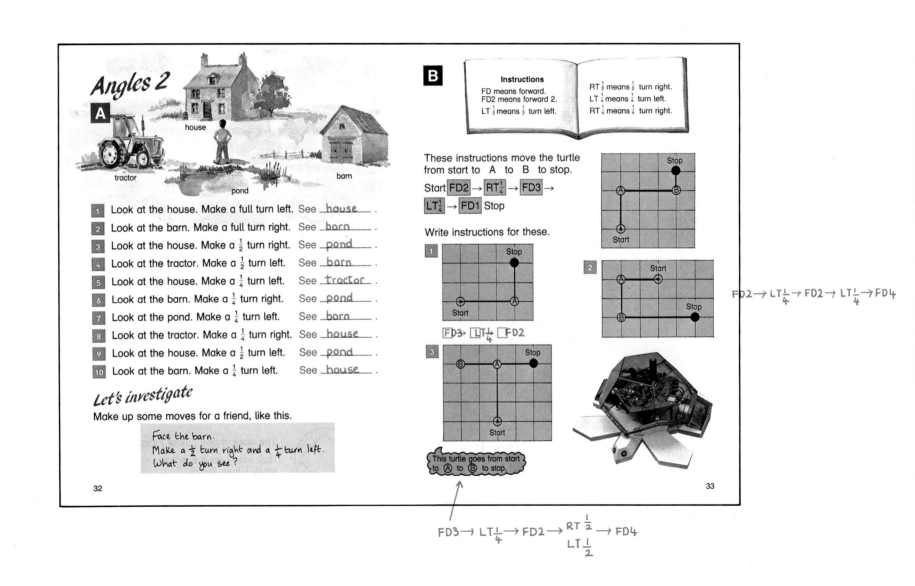

Angles 2

A

house

tractor

pond

barn

1 Look at the house. Make a full turn left. See __house__ .
2 Look at the barn. Make a full turn right. See __barn__ .
3 Look at the house. Make a $\frac{1}{2}$ turn right. See __pond__ .
4 Look at the tractor. Make a $\frac{1}{2}$ turn left. See __barn__ .
5 Look at the house. Make a $\frac{1}{4}$ turn left. See __tractor__ .
6 Look at the barn. Make a $\frac{1}{4}$ turn right. See __pond__ .
7 Look at the pond. Make a $\frac{1}{4}$ turn left. See __barn__ .
8 Look at the tractor. Make a $\frac{1}{4}$ turn right. See __house__ .
9 Look at the house. Make a $\frac{1}{2}$ turn left. See __pond__ .
10 Look at the barn. Make a $\frac{1}{4}$ turn left. See __house__ .

Let's investigate

Make up some moves for a friend, like this.

Face the barn.
Make a $\frac{1}{2}$ turn right and a $\frac{1}{4}$ turn left.
What do you see?

32

B

Instructions

FD means forward.
FD2 means forward 2.
LT $\frac{1}{2}$ means $\frac{1}{2}$ turn left.

RT $\frac{1}{2}$ means $\frac{1}{2}$ turn right.
LT $\frac{1}{4}$ means $\frac{1}{4}$ turn left.
RT $\frac{1}{4}$ means $\frac{1}{4}$ turn right.

These instructions move the turtle from start to Ⓐ to Ⓑ to stop.

Start FD2 → RT$\frac{1}{4}$ → FD3 →
LT$\frac{1}{4}$ → FD1 Stop

Write instructions for these.

1
FD3 → LT$\frac{1}{4}$ → FD2

2
FD2 → LT$\frac{1}{4}$ → FD2 → LT$\frac{1}{4}$ → FD4

3

This turtle goes from start to Ⓐ to Ⓑ to stop.

FD3 → LT$\frac{1}{4}$ → FD2 → RT$\frac{1}{2}$ → FD4
LT$\frac{1}{2}$

33

Let's investigate

Draw turtle paths of your own.
Show where the turtle starts and stops.

Write instructions for the paths.

FD5 → RT¼ → FD5 →
RT¼ → FD5 → RT¼ → FD5

C The turtle drew this square.

1 Write the instructions.

Start □ → □ → □ → □
→ □ → □ → □ Stop

Stop ⊕
Start

2 Follow these instructions.

Start FD2 → LT¼ → FD5 → LT¼ →
FD2 → LT¼ → FD5 Stop

Rectangle

Draw the shape. What is it?

Let's investigate

Use squared paper.

Keep to the lines.

Draw a six-sided shape.

Write different ways for the turtle to draw the same six-sided shape.

34

Number 11

A

This square is from China.
It is very old.

1 Now it looks like this.
Copy it and finish it.

4	9	2
3	5	7
8	1	6

2 Add each line.
What do you get? 15
This is the magic number.

N.B. The small circles show the numbers

Copy these squares. Finish them.

3

3	8	7
10	6	2
5	4	9

Magic number 18

4

11	6	7
4	8	12
9	10	5

These are magic squares

Magic number 24

Find the patterns. Write the numbers.

5 3 13 23 33 43 53 63

6 9 19 29 39 49 59 69

7 38 48 58 68 78 88 98

8 15 25 35 45 55 65 75

35

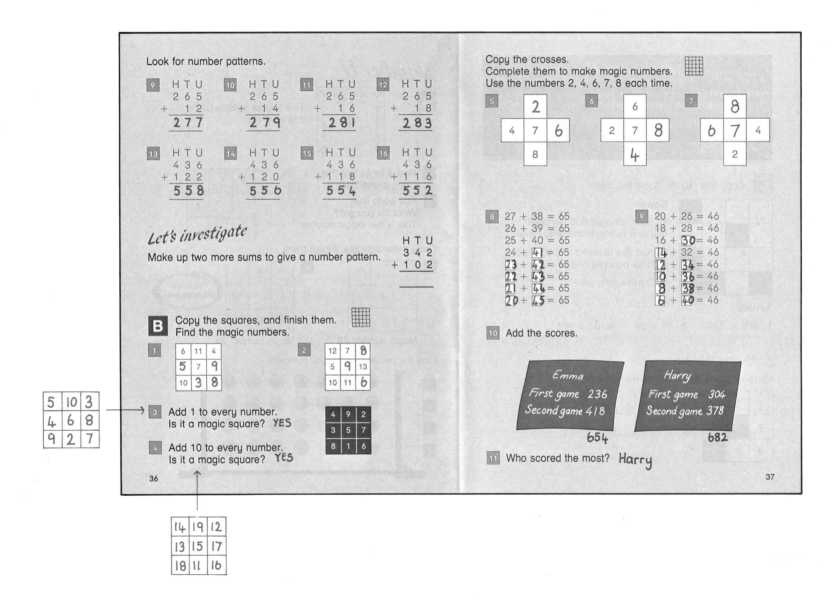

Look for number patterns.

9	H T U
	2 6 5
	+ 1 2
	2 7 7

10	H T U
	2 6 5
	+ 1 4
	2 7 9

11	H T U
	2 6 5
	+ 1 6
	2 8 1

12	H T U
	2 6 5
	+ 1 8
	2 8 3

13	H T U
	4 3 6
	+ 1 2 2
	5 5 8

14	H T U
	4 3 6
	+ 1 2 0
	5 5 6

15	H T U
	4 3 6
	+ 1 1 8
	5 5 4

16	H T U
	4 3 6
	+ 1 1 6
	5 5 2

Let's investigate

Make up two more sums to give a number pattern.

H T U
3 4 2
+ 1 0 2
———

B Copy the squares, and finish them.
Find the magic numbers.

1.
6	11	4
5	7	**9**
10	**3**	**8**

2.
12	7	**8**
5	**9**	13
10	11	**6**

5	10	3
4	6	8
9	2	7

3. Add 1 to every number.
Is it a magic square? **YES**

4	9	2
3	5	7
8	1	6

4. Add 10 to every number.
Is it a magic square? **YES**

14	19	12
13	15	17
18	11	16

36

Copy the crosses.
Complete them to make magic numbers.
Use the numbers 2, 4, 6, 7, 8 each time.

5.
	2	
4	7	6
	8	

6.
	6	
2	7	8
	4	

7.
		8
6	7	4
	2	

8.
27 + 38 = 65
26 + 39 = 65
25 + 40 = 65
24 + **4** = 65
23 + **42** = 65
22 + **43** = 65
21 + **44** = 65
20 + **45** = 65

9.
20 + 26 = 46
18 + 28 = 46
16 + **30** = 46
14 + 32 = 46
12 + **34** = 46
10 + **36** = 46
8 + **38** = 46
6 + **40** = 46

10. Add the scores.

Emma
First game   236
Second game 418
654

Harry
First game   304
Second game 378
682

11. Who scored the most? **Harry**

37

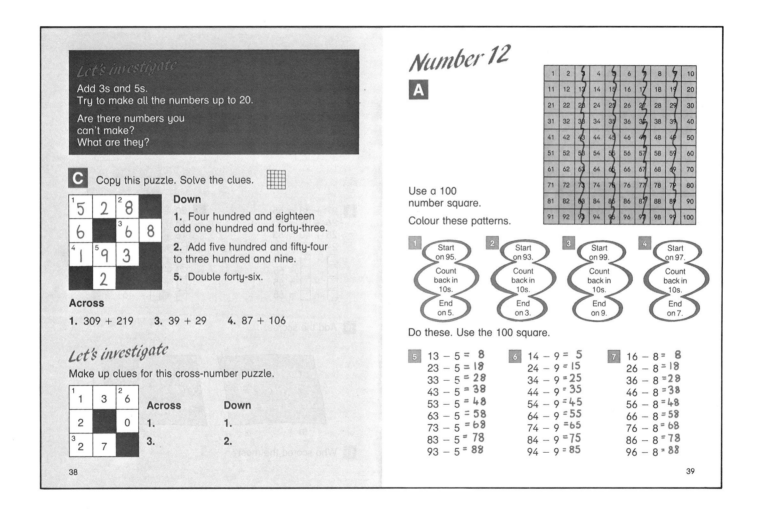

Let's investigate

Add 3s and 5s.
Try to make all the numbers up to 20.

Are there numbers you
can't make?
What are they?

C Copy this puzzle. Solve the clues.

5	2	8
6		6	8
1	9	3
	2	

Down

1. Four hundred and eighteen
add one hundred and forty-three.

2. Add five hundred and fifty-four
to three hundred and nine.

5. Double forty-six.

Across

1. 309 + 219   **3.** 39 + 29   **4.** 87 + 106

Let's investigate

Make up clues for this cross-number puzzle.

1	3	6
2		0
2	7	

Across   **Down**
1.   **1.**
3.   **2.**

38

Number 12

A

1	2	3	4	5	6	7	8	9	10
11	12	13	14	15	16	17	18	19	20
21	22	23	24	25	26	27	28	29	30
31	32	33	34	35	36	37	38	39	40
41	42	43	44	45	46	47	48	49	50
51	52	53	54	55	56	57	58	59	60
61	62	63	64	65	66	67	68	69	70
71	72	73	74	75	76	77	78	79	80
81	82	83	84	85	86	87	88	89	90
91	92	93	94	95	96	97	98	99	100

Use a 100
number square.

Colour these patterns.

1 Start on 95. Count back in 10s. End on 5.

2 Start on 93. Count back in 10s. End on 3.

3 Start on 99. Count back in 10s. End on 9.

4 Start on 97. Count back in 10s. End on 7.

Do these. Use the 100 square.

5
13 − 5 = 8
23 − 5 = 18
33 − 5 = 28
43 − 5 = 38
53 − 5 = 48
63 − 5 = 58
73 − 5 = 68
83 − 5 = 78
93 − 5 = 88

6
14 − 9 = 5
24 − 9 = 15
34 − 9 = 25
44 − 9 = 35
54 − 9 = 45
64 − 9 = 55
74 − 9 = 65
84 − 9 = 75
94 − 9 = 85

7
16 − 8 = 8
26 − 8 = 18
36 − 8 = 28
46 − 8 = 38
56 − 8 = 48
66 − 8 = 58
76 − 8 = 68
86 − 8 = 78
96 − 8 = 88

39

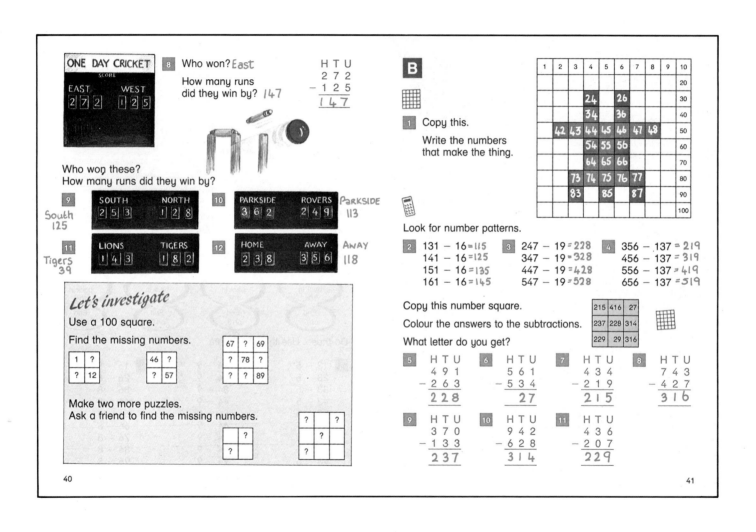

ONE DAY CRICKET
SCORE

EAST	WEST
2 7 2	1 2 5

8 Who won? East

How many runs
did they win by? 147

```
  H T U
  2 7 2
- 1 2 5
  1 4 7
```

Who won these?
How many runs did they win by?

9 SOUTH | NORTH
2 5 3 | 1 2 8

South 125

10 PARKSIDE | ROVERS
3 6 2 | 2 4 9

Parkside 113

11 LIONS | TIGERS
1 4 3 | 1 8 2

Tigers 39

12 HOME | AWAY
2 3 8 | 3 5 6

Away 118

Let's investigate

Use a 100 square.

Find the missing numbers.

1	?
?	12

46	?
?	57

67	?	69
?	78	?
?	?	89

Make two more puzzles.
Ask a friend to find the missing numbers.

B

1 Copy this.

Write the numbers
that make the thing.

1	2	3	4	5	6	7	8	9	10
									20
			24		26				30
			34		36				40
	42	43	44	45	46	47	48		50
			54	55	56				60
			64	65	66				70
		73	74	75	76	77			80
		83		85		87			90
									100

Look for number patterns.

2 131 − 16 = 115
   141 − 16 = 125
   151 − 16 = 135
   161 − 16 = 145

3 247 − 19 = 228
   347 − 19 = 328
   447 − 19 = 428
   547 − 19 = 528

4 356 − 137 = 219
   456 − 137 = 319
   556 − 137 = 419
   656 − 137 = 519

Copy this number square.

Colour the answers to the subtractions.

What letter do you get?

215	416	27
237	228	314
229	29	316

5
```
  H T U
  4 9 1
- 2 6 3
  2 2 8
```

6
```
  H T U
  5 6 1
- 5 3 4
    2 7
```

7
```
  H T U
  4 3 4
- 2 1 9
  2 1 5
```

8
```
  H T U
  7 4 3
- 4 2 7
  3 1 6
```

9
```
  H T U
  3 7 0
- 1 3 3
  2 3 7
```

10
```
  H T U
  9 4 2
- 6 2 8
  3 1 4
```

11
```
  H T U
  4 3 6
- 2 0 7
  2 2 9
```

40

41

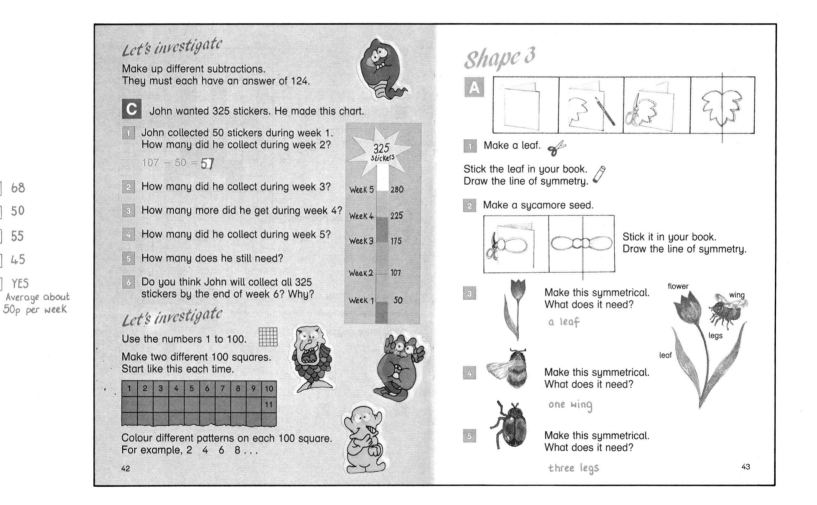

Let's investigate

Make up different subtractions.
They must each have an answer of 124.

C   John wanted 325 stickers. He made this chart.

1   John collected 50 stickers during week 1.
How many did he collect during week 2?

107 – 50 = 57

2   How many did he collect during week 3?

3   How many more did he get during week 4?

4   How many did he collect during week 5?

5   How many does he still need?

6   Do you think John will collect all 325 stickers by the end of week 6? Why?

325 stickers

Week 5	280
Week 4	225
Week 3	175
Week 2	107
Week 1	50

Let's investigate

Use the numbers 1 to 100.

Make two different 100 squares.
Start like this each time.

1	2	3	4	5	6	7	8	9	10
									11

Colour different patterns on each 100 square.
For example, 2 4 6 8...

42

Shape 3

A

1   Make a leaf.

Stick the leaf in your book.
Draw the line of symmetry.

2   Make a sycamore seed.

Stick it in your book.
Draw the line of symmetry.

3   Make this symmetrical.
What does it need?

a leaf

flower
wing
legs
leaf

4   Make this symmetrical.
What does it need?

one wing

5   Make this symmetrical.
What does it need?

three legs

43

(margin answers)

2   68

3   50

4   55

5   45

6   YES
Average about
50p per week

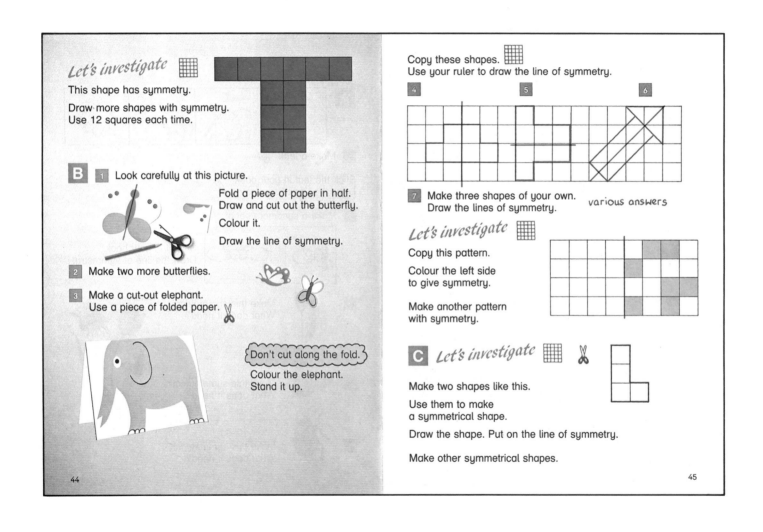

Let's investigate

This shape has symmetry.

Draw more shapes with symmetry.
Use 12 squares each time.

B

1   Look carefully at this picture.

Fold a piece of paper in half.
Draw and cut out the butterfly.

Colour it.

Draw the line of symmetry.

2   Make two more butterflies.

3   Make a cut-out elephant.
Use a piece of folded paper.

Don't cut along the fold.

Colour the elephant.
Stand it up.

44

Copy these shapes.
Use your ruler to draw the line of symmetry.

4   5   6

7   Make three shapes of your own.
Draw the lines of symmetry.   various answers

Let's investigate

Copy this pattern.

Colour the left side
to give symmetry.

Make another pattern
with symmetry.

C   *Let's investigate*

Make two shapes like this.

Use them to make
a symmetrical shape.

Draw the shape. Put on the line of symmetry.

Make other symmetrical shapes.

45

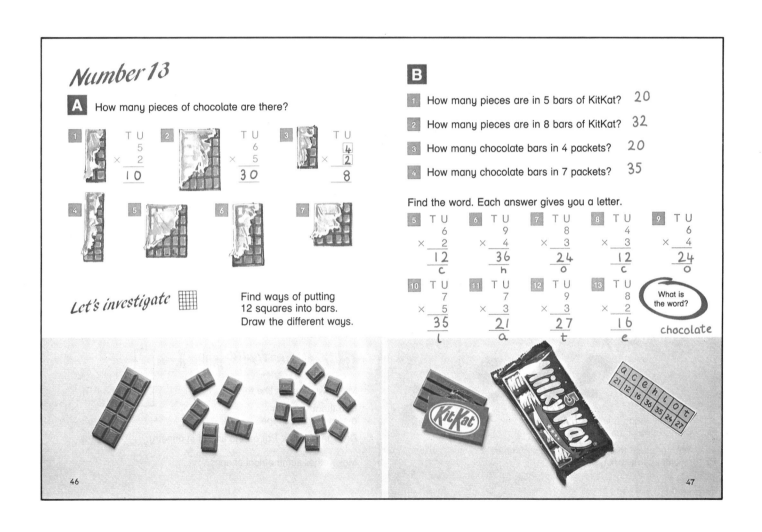

Number 13

A How many pieces of chocolate are there?

1.
```
  T U
    5
×   2
─────
  1 0
```

2.
```
  T U
    6
×   5
─────
  3 0
```

3.
```
  T U
    4
×   2
─────
    8
```

Let's investigate

Find ways of putting 12 squares into bars. Draw the different ways.

B

1. How many pieces are in 5 bars of KitKat? 20
2. How many pieces are in 8 bars of KitKat? 32
3. How many chocolate bars in 4 packets? 20
4. How many chocolate bars in 7 packets? 35

Find the word. Each answer gives you a letter.

5.
```
  T U
    6
×   2
─────
  1 2
   c
```

6.
```
  T U
    9
×   4
─────
  3 6
   h
```

7.
```
  T U
    8
×   3
─────
  2 4
   o
```

8.
```
  T U
    4
×   3
─────
  1 2
   c
```

9.
```
  T U
    6
×   4
─────
  2 4
   o
```

10.
```
  T U
    7
×   5
─────
  3 5
   l
```

11.
```
  T U
    7
×   3
─────
  2 1
   a
```

12.
```
  T U
    9
×   3
─────
  2 7
   t
```

13.
```
  T U
    8
×   2
─────
  1 6
   e
```

What is the word?

chocolate

a	c	e	h	l	o	t
21	12	16	36	35	24	27

46

47

4.
```
  T U
    9
×   2
─────
  1 8
```

5.
```
  T U
    5
×   5
─────
  2 5
```

6.
```
  T U
    6
×   3
─────
  1 8
```

7.
```
  T U
    4
×   4
─────
  1 6
```

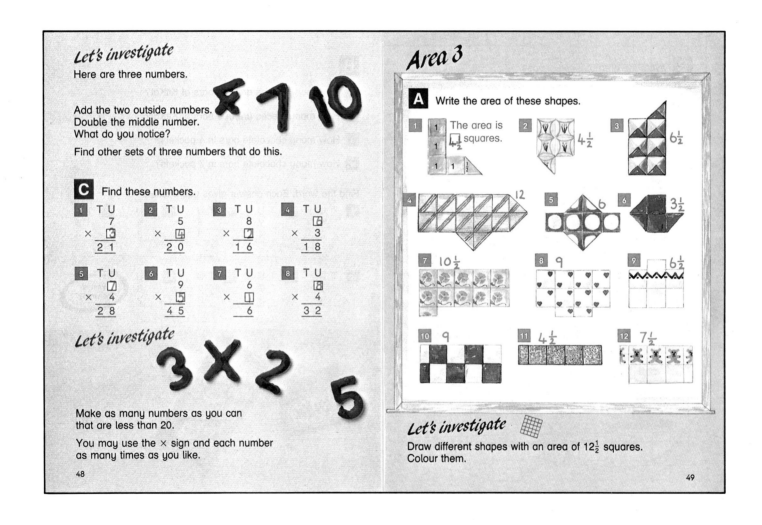

Let's investigate

Here are three numbers.

5 7 10

Add the two outside numbers.
Double the middle number.
What do you notice?

Find other sets of three numbers that do this.

C   Find these numbers.

1	T U
	7
×	☐
	2 1

2	T U
	5
×	☐
	2 0

3	T U
	8
×	☐
	1 6

4	T U
	☐
×	3
	1 8

5	T U
	☐
×	4
	2 8

6	T U
	9
×	☐
	4 5

7	T U
	6
×	☐
	6

8	T U
	☐
×	4
	3 2

Let's investigate

3 × 2 5

Make as many numbers as you can
that are less than 20.

You may use the × sign and each number
as many times as you like.

48

Area 3

A   Write the area of these shapes.

1. | 1 | The area is ☐ squares.
   | 1 |
   | 1 | 1 | 1½

2. 4½

3. 6½

4. 12

5. 6

6. 3½

7. 10½

8. 9

9. 6½

10. 9

11. 4½

12. 7½

Let's investigate

Draw different shapes with an area of 12½ squares.
Colour them.

49

1 $12\frac{1}{2}$

2 10

3 $6\frac{1}{2}$

4 23

5 $15\frac{1}{2}$

6 12

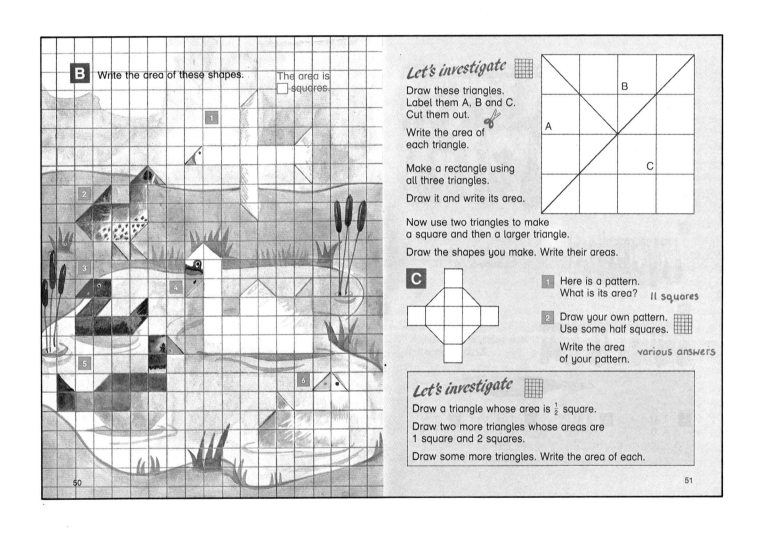

B Write the area of these shapes.

The area is ☐ squares.

Let's investigate

Draw these triangles.
Label them A, B and C.
Cut them out.

Write the area of
each triangle.

Make a rectangle using
all three triangles.

Draw it and write its area.

Now use two triangles to make
a square and then a larger triangle.

Draw the shapes you make. Write their areas.

C

1 Here is a pattern.
   What is its area? *11 squares*

2 Draw your own pattern.
   Use some half squares.

   Write the area
   of your pattern. *various answers*

Let's investigate

Draw a triangle whose area is $\frac{1}{2}$ square.

Draw two more triangles whose areas are
1 square and 2 squares.

Draw some more triangles. Write the area of each.

50

51

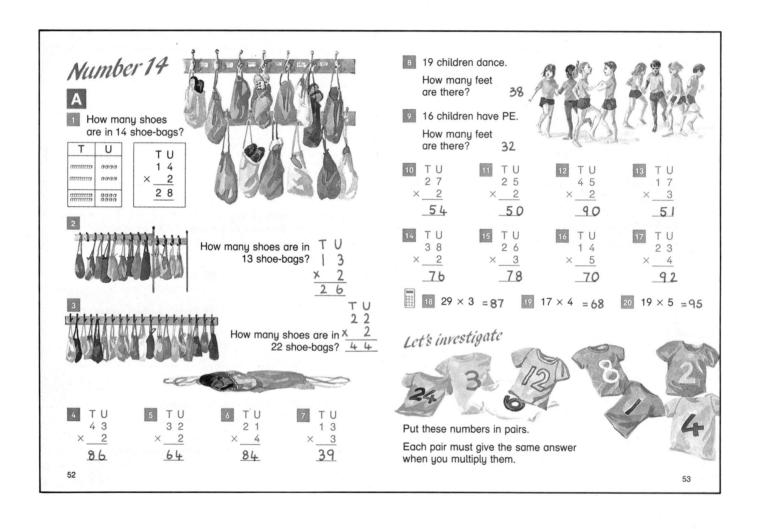

Number 14

A

1 How many shoes are in 14 shoe-bags?

T	U
ᴄᴄᴄᴄᴄᴄᴄ	ᴏᴏᴏᴏ
ᴄᴄᴄᴄᴄᴄᴄ	ᴏᴏᴏᴏ
ᴄᴄᴄᴄᴄᴄᴄ	ᴏᴏᴏᴏ

```
  T U
  1 4
×   2
  2 8
```

2 How many shoes are in 13 shoe-bags?

```
  T U
  1 3
×   2
  2 6
```

How many shoes are in 22 shoe-bags?

```
  T U
  2 2
×   2
  4 4
```

4
```
  T U
  4 3
×   2
  8 6
```

5
```
  T U
  3 2
×   2
  6 4
```

6
```
  T U
  2 1
×   4
  8 4
```

7
```
  T U
  1 3
×   3
  3 9
```

8 19 children dance. How many feet are there? 38

9 16 children have PE. How many feet are there? 32

10
```
  T U
  2 7
×   2
  5 4
```

11
```
  T U
  2 5
×   2
  5 0
```

12
```
  T U
  4 5
×   2
  9 0
```

13
```
  T U
  1 7
×   3
  5 1
```

14
```
  T U
  3 8
×   2
  7 6
```

15
```
  T U
  2 6
×   3
  7 8
```

16
```
  T U
  1 4
×   5
  7 0
```

17
```
  T U
  2 3
×   4
  9 2
```

18 $29 \times 3 = 87$ **19** $17 \times 4 = 68$ **20** $19 \times 5 = 95$

Let's investigate

Put these numbers in pairs.

Each pair must give the same answer when you multiply them.

24 3 12 6 8 1 2 4

52   53

B

This school has 4 classes.
There are 24 children
in each class.

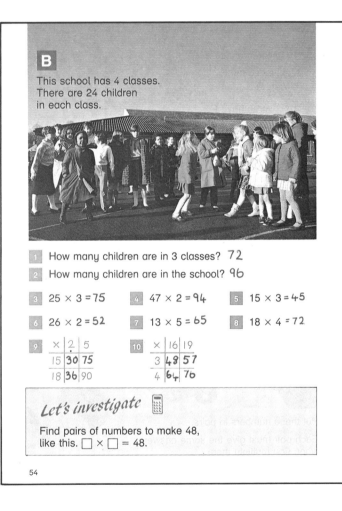

1. How many children are in 3 classes? 72
2. How many children are in the school? 96

3. 25 × 3 = 75   4. 47 × 2 = 94   5. 15 × 3 = 45

6. 26 × 2 = 52   7. 13 × 5 = 65   8. 18 × 4 = 72

9.

×	2	5
15	30	75
18	36	90

10.

×	16	19
3	48	57
4	64	76

Let's investigate

Find pairs of numbers to make 48,
like this. ☐ × ☐ = 48.

54

C

The children in Class
4 are in groups of 3.

Each child needs
2 paintbrushes,
3 pieces of paper
and 5 crayons.

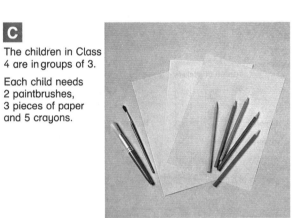

1. How many paintbrushes for 3 groups?   18
2. How many pieces of paper for 5 groups?   45
3. How many crayons for 6 groups?   90

Let's investigate

Use three different numbers.
Multiply them together.
The answer must be less than 25.

What sets of numbers can you find?

55

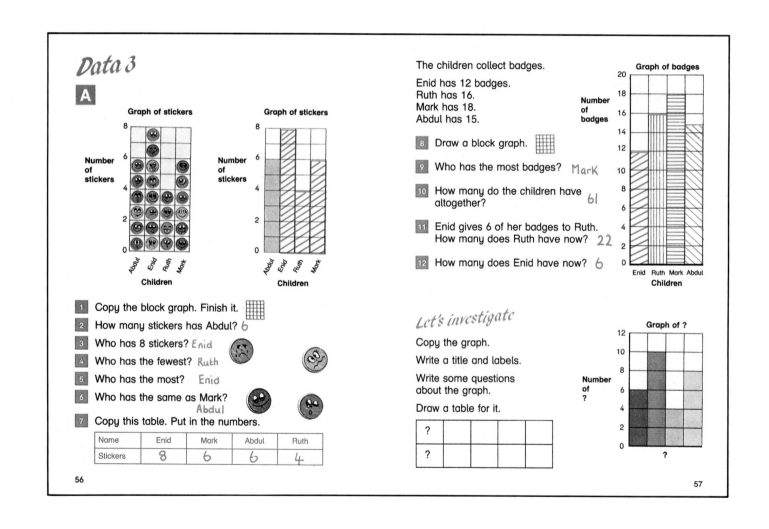

Data 3

A

Graph of stickers

Number of stickers

8
6
4
2
0

Abdul Enid Ruth Mark

Children

Graph of stickers

Number of stickers

8
6
4
2
0

Abdul Enid Ruth Mark

Children

1 Copy the block graph. Finish it.
2 How many stickers has Abdul? 6
3 Who has 8 stickers? Enid
4 Who has the fewest? Ruth
5 Who has the most? Enid
6 Who has the same as Mark?
    Abdul
7 Copy this table. Put in the numbers.

Name	Enid	Mark	Abdul	Ruth
Stickers	8	6	6	4

56

The children collect badges.

Enid has 12 badges.
Ruth has 16.
Mark has 18.
Abdul has 15.

8 Draw a block graph.

9 Who has the most badges? Mark

10 How many do the children have altogether? 61

11 Enid gives 6 of her badges to Ruth. How many does Ruth have now? 22

12 How many does Enid have now? 6

Graph of badges

Number of badges

20
18
16
14
12
10
8
6
4
2
0

Enid Ruth Mark Abdul

Children

Let's investigate

Copy the graph.

Write a title and labels.

Write some questions about the graph.

Draw a table for it.

?				
?				

Graph of ?

Number of ?

12
10
8
6
4
2
0

?

57

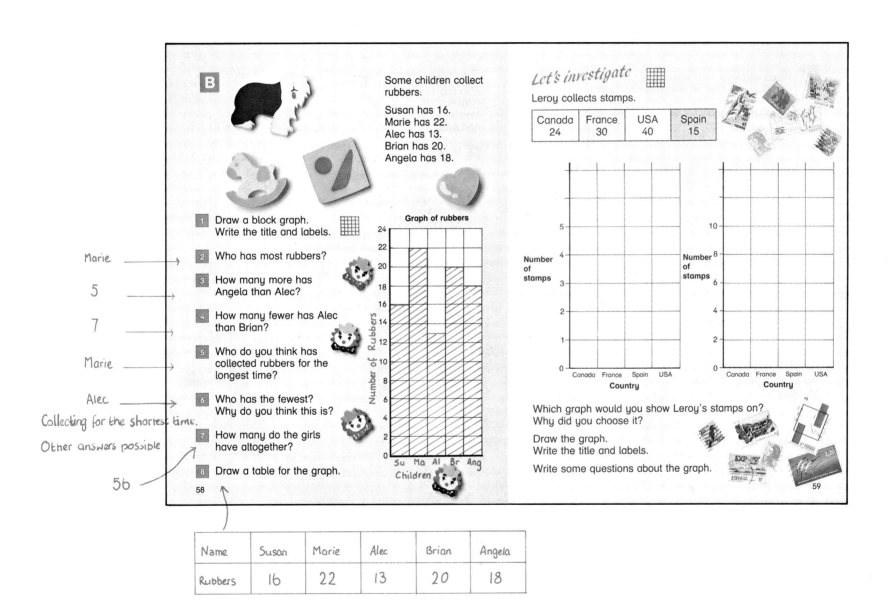

B

Some children collect rubbers.

Susan has 16.
Marie has 22.
Alec has 13.
Brian has 20.
Angela has 18.

1 Draw a block graph. Write the title and labels.

2 Who has most rubbers?

Marie

3 How many more has Angela than Alec?

5

4 How many fewer has Alec than Brian?

7

5 Who do you think has collected rubbers for the longest time?

Marie

6 Who has the fewest? Why do you think this is?

Alec
Collecting for the shortest time.
Other answers possible

7 How many do the girls have altogether?

56

8 Draw a table for the graph.

58

Graph of rubbers

(bar graph: vertical axis "Number of Rubbers" 0–24, horizontal axis "Children" Su Ma Al Br Ang)

Name	Susan	Marie	Alec	Brian	Angela
Rubbers	16	22	13	20	18

Let's investigate

Leroy collects stamps.

Canada 24	France 30	USA 40	Spain 15

(two empty grid graphs with vertical axis "Number of stamps", horizontal axis "Country": Canada France Spain USA)

Which graph would you show Leroy's stamps on? Why did you choose it?

Draw the graph. Write the title and labels.

Write some questions about the graph.

59

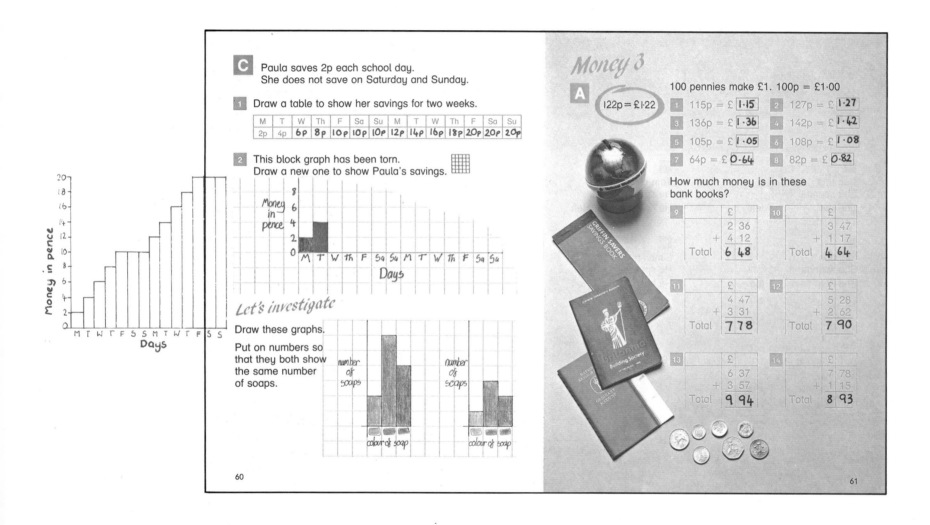

C Paula saves 2p each school day.
She does not save on Saturday and Sunday.

1 Draw a table to show her savings for two weeks.

M	T	W	Th	F	Sa	Su	M	T	W	Th	F	Sa	Su
2p	4p	6p	8p	10p	10p	10p	12p	14p	16p	18p	20p	20p	20p

2 This block graph has been torn.
Draw a new one to show Paula's savings.

Money in pence

Let's investigate

Draw these graphs.

Put on numbers so that they both show the same number of soaps.

number of soaps   number of soaps

colour of soap   colour of soap

60

Money 3

A   122p = £1·22   100 pennies make £1. 100p = £1·00

1 115p = £ **1·15**   **2** 127p = £ **1·27**

3 136p = £ **1·36**   **4** 142p = £ **1·42**

5 105p = £ **1·05**   **6** 108p = £ **1·08**

7 64p = £ **0·64**   **8** 82p = £ **0·82**

How much money is in these bank books?

9	£	
	2	36
+	4	12
Total	6	48

10	£	
	3	47
+	1	17
Total	4	64

11	£	
	4	47
+	3	31
Total	7	78

12	£	
	5	28
+	2	62
Total	7	90

13	£	
	6	37
+	3	57
Total	9	94

14	£	
	7	78
+	1	15
Total	8	93

61

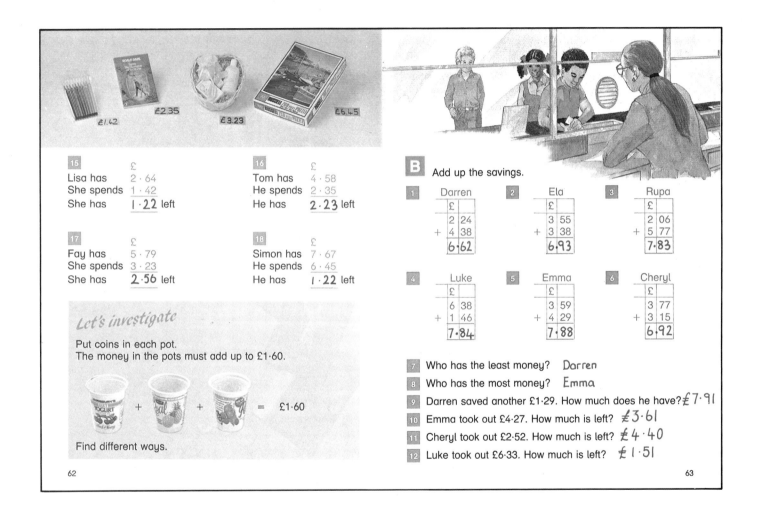

£1.42   £2.35   £3.23   £6.45

15
£
Lisa has   2 · 64
She spends   1 · 42
She has   **1 · 22** left

16
£
Tom has   4 · 58
He spends   2 · 35
He has   **2 · 23** left

17
£
Fay has   5 · 79
She spends   3 · 23
She has   **2 · 56** left

18
£
Simon has   7 · 67
He spends   6 · 45
He has   **1 · 22** left

Let's investigate

Put coins in each pot.
The money in the pots must add up to £1·60.

▢ + ▢ + ▢ = £1·60

Find different ways.

62

B Add up the savings.

1 Darren
£	
2	24
+ 4	38
6·62	

2 Ela
£	
3	55
+ 3	38
6·93	

3 Rupa
£	
2	06
+ 5	77
7·83	

4 Luke
£	
6	38
+ 1	46
7·84	

5 Emma
£	
3	59
+ 4	29
7·88	

6 Cheryl
£	
3	77
+ 3	15
6·92	

7 Who has the least money?   Darren

8 Who has the most money?   Emma

9 Darren saved another £1·29. How much does he have? £7·91

10 Emma took out £4·27. How much is left? £3·61

11 Cheryl took out £2·52. How much is left? £4·40

12 Luke took out £6·33. How much is left? £1·51

63

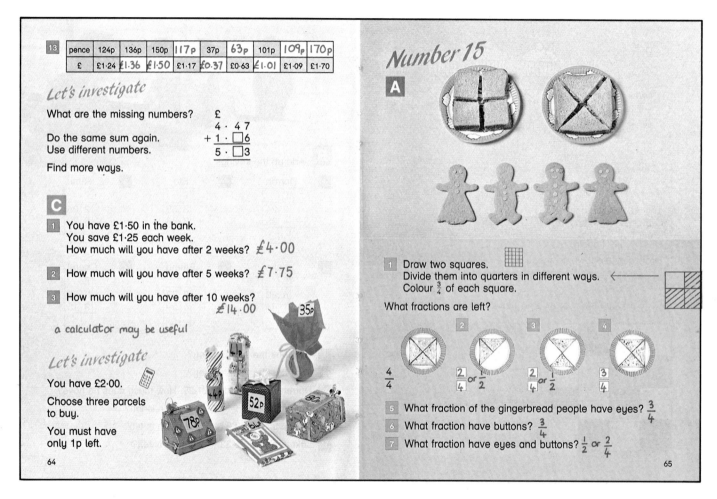

13	pence	124p	136p	150p	117p	37p	63p	101p	109p	170p
	£	£1·24	£1·36	£1·50	£1·17	£0·37	£0·63	£1·01	£1·09	£1·70

Let's investigate

What are the missing numbers?

Do the same sum again.
Use different numbers.

$$\begin{array}{r} £ \\ 4 \cdot 47 \\ + \ 1 \cdot \square 6 \\ \hline 5 \cdot \square 3 \end{array}$$

Find more ways.

C

1. You have £1·50 in the bank.
   You save £1·25 each week.
   How much will you have after 2 weeks? £4·00

2. How much will you have after 5 weeks? £7·75

3. How much will you have after 10 weeks? £14·00

a calculator may be useful

Let's investigate

You have £2·00.

Choose three parcels to buy.

You must have only 1p left.

64

Number 15

A

1. Draw two squares.
   Divide them into quarters in different ways.
   Colour $\frac{3}{4}$ of each square.

What fractions are left?

1	2	3	4
$\frac{4}{4}$	$\frac{2}{4}$ or $\frac{1}{2}$	$\frac{2}{4}$ or $\frac{1}{2}$	$\frac{3}{4}$

5. What fraction of the gingerbread people have eyes? $\frac{3}{4}$
6. What fraction have buttons? $\frac{3}{4}$
7. What fraction have eyes and buttons? $\frac{1}{2}$ or $\frac{2}{4}$

colouring may vary

65

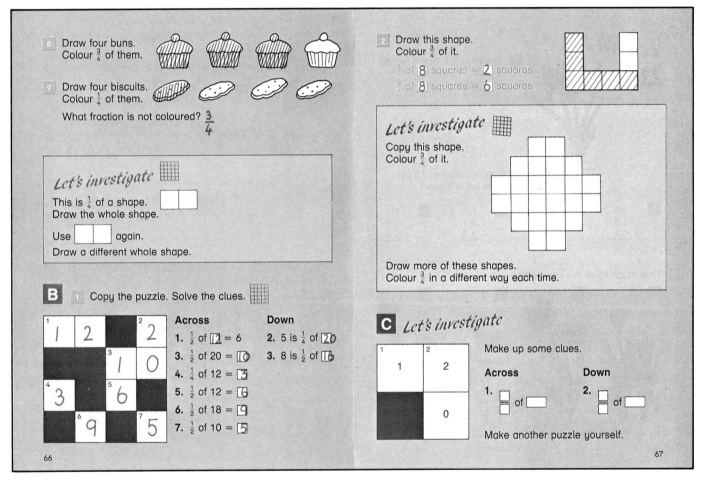

8 Draw four buns.
Colour $\frac{3}{4}$ of them.

9 Draw four biscuits.
Colour $\frac{1}{4}$ of them.

What fraction is not coloured? $\frac{3}{4}$

Let's investigate

This is $\frac{1}{4}$ of a shape.
Draw the whole shape.

Use [ ][ ] again.
Draw a different whole shape.

B **1** Copy the puzzle. Solve the clues.

1	2		2
		3	0
3	5		
	6		7

Across
1. $\frac{1}{2}$ of 12 = 6
3. $\frac{1}{2}$ of 20 = 10
4. $\frac{1}{4}$ of 12 = 3
5. $\frac{1}{2}$ of 12 = 6
6. $\frac{1}{2}$ of 18 = 9
7. $\frac{1}{2}$ of 10 = 5

Down
2. 5 is $\frac{1}{4}$ of 20
3. 8 is $\frac{1}{2}$ of 16

66

2 Draw this shape.
Colour $\frac{3}{4}$ of it.

$\frac{1}{4}$ of 8 squares = 2 squares
$\frac{3}{4}$ of 8 squares = 6 squares

Any 6 Squares
may be coloured

Let's investigate

Copy this shape.
Colour $\frac{3}{4}$ of it.

Draw more of these shapes.
Colour $\frac{3}{4}$ in a different way each time.

C *Let's investigate*

1	2
	0

Make up some clues.

Across
1. $\frac{\square}{\square}$ of $\square$

Down
2. $\frac{\square}{\square}$ of $\square$

Make another puzzle yourself.

67

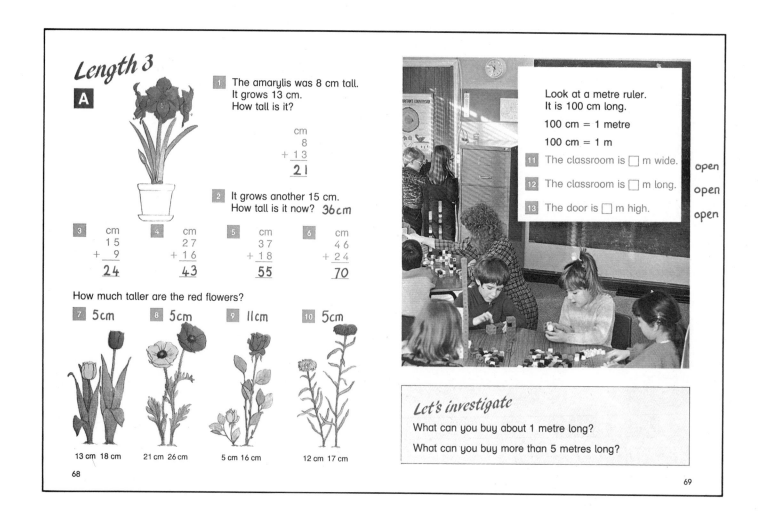

Length 3

A

1 The amarylis was 8 cm tall.
It grows 13 cm.
How tall is it?

$$\begin{array}{r} \text{cm} \\ 8 \\ +\ 13 \\ \hline 21 \end{array}$$

2 It grows another 15 cm.
How tall is it now? **36cm**

3
$$\begin{array}{r} \text{cm} \\ 15 \\ +\ 9 \\ \hline \underline{24} \end{array}$$

4
$$\begin{array}{r} \text{cm} \\ 27 \\ +\ 16 \\ \hline \underline{43} \end{array}$$

5
$$\begin{array}{r} \text{cm} \\ 37 \\ +\ 18 \\ \hline \underline{55} \end{array}$$

6
$$\begin{array}{r} \text{cm} \\ 46 \\ +\ 24 \\ \hline \underline{70} \end{array}$$

How much taller are the red flowers?

7 5cm　**8** 5cm　**9** 11cm　**10** 5cm

13 cm　18 cm　　21 cm　26 cm　　5 cm　16 cm　　12 cm　17 cm

68

Look at a metre ruler.
It is 100 cm long.

100 cm = 1 metre

100 cm = 1 m

11 The classroom is ☐ m wide.　open

12 The classroom is ☐ m long.　open

13 The door is ☐ m high.　open

Let's investigate

What can you buy about 1 metre long?

What can you buy more than 5 metres long?

69

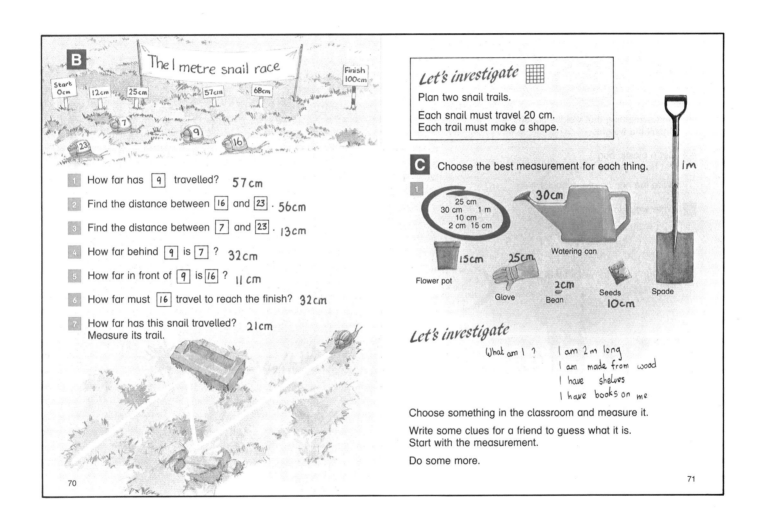

B The 1 metre snail race

Start 0cm   12cm   25cm   57cm   68cm   Finish 100cm

1 How far has [9] travelled? 57 cm

2 Find the distance between [16] and [23]. 56 cm

3 Find the distance between [7] and [23]. 13 cm

4 How far behind [9] is [7]? 32 cm

5 How far in front of [9] is [16]? 11 cm

6 How far must [16] travel to reach the finish? 32 cm

7 How far has this snail travelled? 21 cm
   Measure its trail.

70

Let's investigate

Plan two snail trails.

Each snail must travel 20 cm.
Each trail must make a shape.

C Choose the best measurement for each thing.

1
25 cm
30 cm   1 m
10 cm
2 cm 15 cm

30cm

Watering can

15cm Flower pot

25cm Glove

2cm Bean

Seeds 10cm

Spade 1m

Let's investigate

What am I ?   I am 2 m long
              I am made from wood
              I have shelves
              I have books on me

Choose something in the classroom and measure it.

Write some clues for a friend to guess what it is.
Start with the measurement.

Do some more.

71

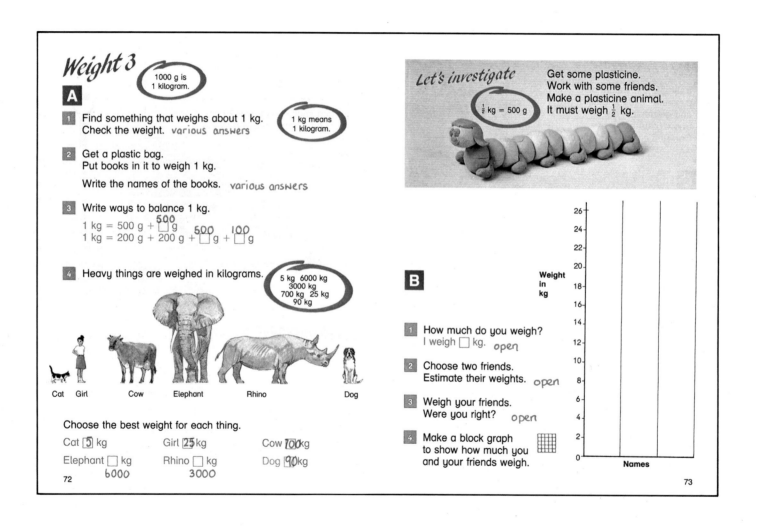

Weight 3

1000 g is 1 kilogram.

A

1. Find something that weighs about 1 kg.
Check the weight.   *various answers*

1 kg means 1 kilogram.

2. Get a plastic bag.
Put books in it to weigh 1 kg.

Write the names of the books.   *various answers*

3. Write ways to balance 1 kg.
1 kg = 500 g + $\boxed{500}$ g
1 kg = 200 g + 200 g + $\boxed{500}$ g + $\boxed{100}$ g

4. Heavy things are weighed in kilograms.

5 kg 6000 kg
3000 kg
700 kg 25 kg
90 kg

Cat   Girl   Cow   Elephant   Rhino   Dog

Choose the best weight for each thing.

Cat $\boxed{5}$ kg   Girl $\boxed{25}$ kg   Cow $\boxed{700}$ kg

Elephant $\boxed{}$ kg   Rhino $\boxed{}$ kg   Dog $\boxed{90}$ kg
6000   *3000*

72

Let's investigate

Get some plasticine.
Work with some friends.
Make a plasticine animal.
It must weigh $\frac{1}{2}$ kg.

$\frac{1}{2}$ kg = 500 g

B

Weight in kg

1. How much do you weigh?
I weigh $\boxed{}$ kg.   *open*

2. Choose two friends.
Estimate their weights.   *open*

3. Weigh your friends.
Were you right?   *open*

4. Make a block graph
to show how much you
and your friends weigh.

26
24
22
20
18
16
14
12
10
8
6
4
2
0

Names

73

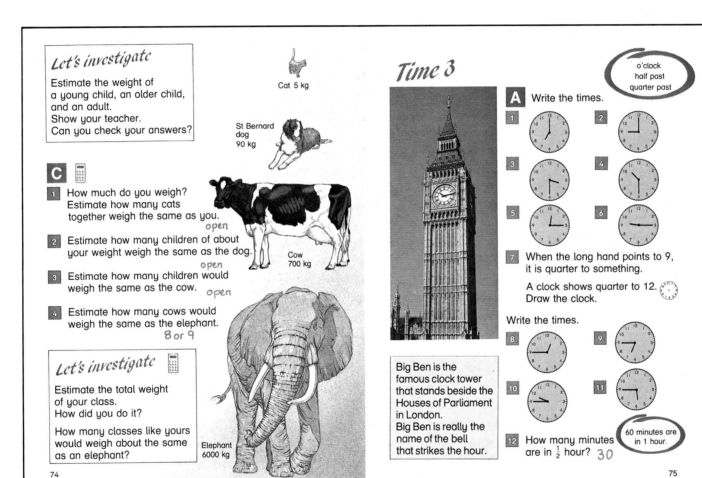

Let's investigate

Estimate the weight of
a young child, an older child,
and an adult.
Show your teacher.
Can you check your answers?

Cat 5 kg

St Bernard
dog
90 kg

C 📱

1 How much do you weigh?
Estimate how many cats
together weigh the same as you.
open

2 Estimate how many children of about
your weight weigh the same as the dog.
open

3 Estimate how many children would
weigh the same as the cow. *open*

4 Estimate how many cows would
weigh the same as the elephant.
8 or 9

Cow
700 kg

Let's investigate 📱

Estimate the total weight
of your class.
How did you do it?

How many classes like yours
would weigh about the same
as an elephant?

Elephant
6000 kg

74

Time 3

Big Ben is the
famous clock tower
that stands beside the
Houses of Parliament
in London.
Big Ben is really the
name of the bell
that strikes the hour.

A Write the times.

*o'clock
half past
quarter past*

1 ⊙ 2 ⊙

3 ⊙ 4 ⊙

5 ⊙ 6 ⊙

7 When the long hand points to 9,
it is quarter to something.

A clock shows quarter to 12. ⊙
Draw the clock.

Write the times.

8 ⊙ 9 ⊙

10 ⊙ 11 ⊙

12 How many minutes
are in ½ hour? *30*

*60 minutes are
in 1 hour.*

75

☐1 7 o'clock

☐2 9 o'clock

☐3 half past 3

☐4 half past 10

☐5 quarter past 12

☐6 quarter past 9

☐8 quarter to 1

☐9 quarter to 7

☐10 quarter to 10

☐11 quarter to 6

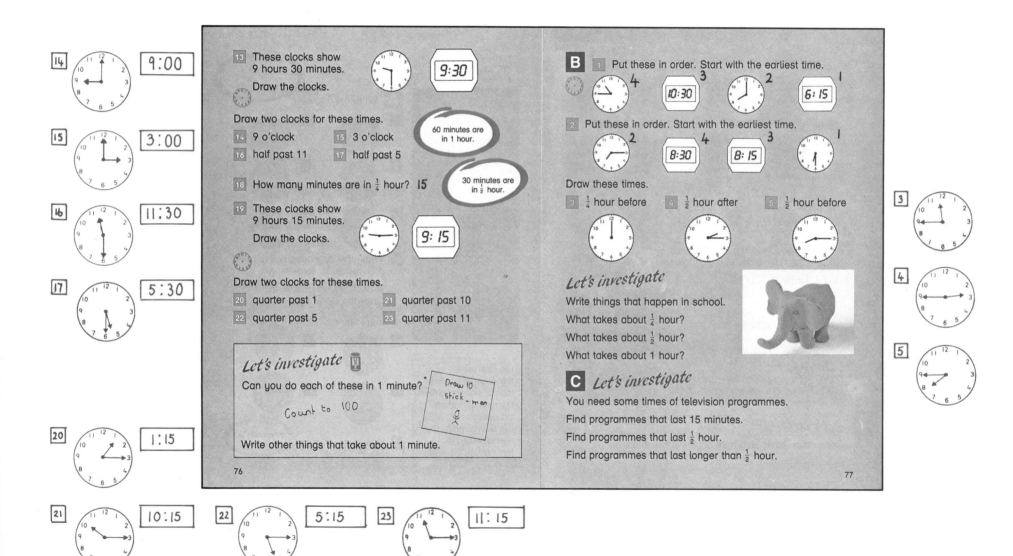

14 9:00

15 3:00

16 11:30

17 5:30

20 1:15

21 10:15

22 5:15

23 11:15

3

4

5

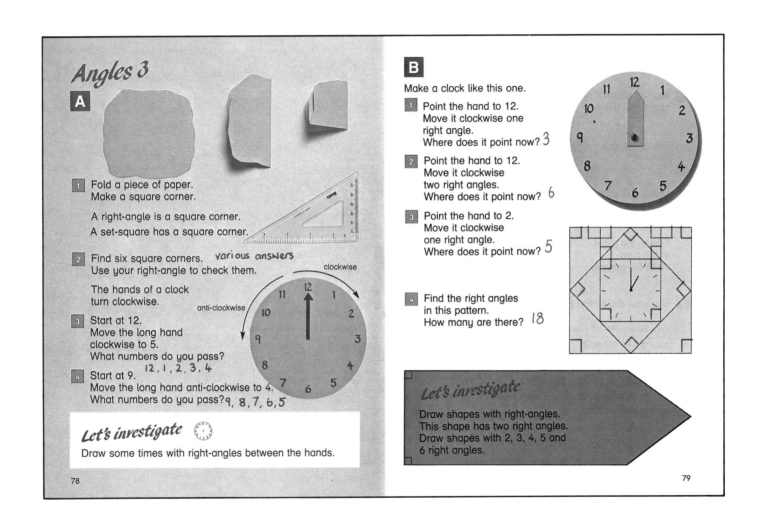

Angles 3

A

1. Fold a piece of paper.
   Make a square corner.

   A right-angle is a square corner.
   A set-square has a square corner.

2. Find six square corners.   *various answers*
   Use your right-angle to check them.

   The hands of a clock
   turn clockwise.

   clockwise
   anti-clockwise

3. Start at 12.
   Move the long hand
   clockwise to 5.
   What numbers do you pass?
   12, 1, 2, 3, 4

4. Start at 9.
   Move the long hand anti-clockwise to 4.
   What numbers do you pass? 9, 8, 7, 6, 5

Let's investigate

Draw some times with right-angles between the hands.

78

B

Make a clock like this one.

1. Point the hand to 12.
   Move it clockwise one
   right angle.
   Where does it point now? 3

2. Point the hand to 12.
   Move it clockwise
   two right angles.
   Where does it point now? 6

3. Point the hand to 2.
   Move it clockwise
   one right angle.
   Where does it point now? 5

4. Find the right angles
   in this pattern.
   How many are there? 18

Let's investigate

Draw shapes with right-angles.
This shape has two right angles.
Draw shapes with 2, 3, 4, 5 and
6 right angles.

79

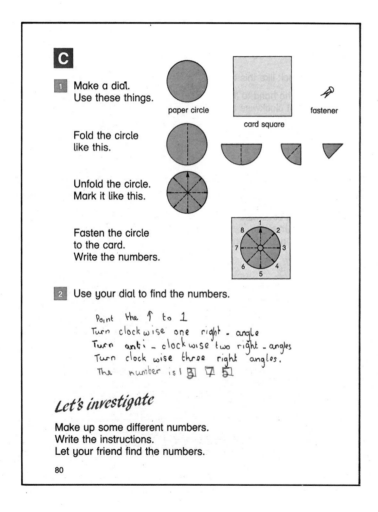

C

1   Make a dial.
    Use these things.

    paper circle   card square   fastener

    Fold the circle
    like this.

    Unfold the circle.
    Mark it like this.

    Fasten the circle
    to the card.
    Write the numbers.

2   Use your dial to find the numbers.

    Point the ↑ to 1
    Turn clockwise one right - angle
    Turn anti - clockwise two right - angles
    Turn clockwise three right angles.
    The number is 1 3 7 5

Let's investigate

Make up some different numbers.
Write the instructions.
Let your friend find the numbers.

Published by the Press Syndicate of the University of Cambridge
The Pitt Building, Trumpington Street, Cambridge CB2 1RP
40 West 20th Street, New York, NY 10011, USA
10 Stamford Road, Oakleigh, Melbourne 3166, Australia

First published 1989

Printed in Great Britain by Scotprint, Musselburgh, Scotland

ISBN 0 521 35830 2

DP